COLLINS POCKET REFERENCE

CARD GAMES

HarperCollins*Publishers*

HarperCollins Publishers
P.O. Box, Glasgow G4 0NB
www.fireandwater.com

A Diagram book first created by Diagram Visual Information
Limited of 195 Kentish Town Road, London NW5 8SY

First published 1994

Reprint 10 9 8 7 6 5 4

ISBN 0 00 470459 2

A catalogue record for this book is available
from the British Library

Printed and bound in Great Britain
by Bath Press

Introduction

Card playing has been a popular pastime for more than 500 years. This long history, and the enormous variety of card games that exist, give card playing its great potential as a plentiful source of entertainment for all ages.

The *Collins Pocket Reference Card Games* is a fascinating two-colour guide to the rules and strategies for over 130 exciting card games and variations. Included are family, children's and patience games, and those that are played for stakes (some of which are suitable only for older players). From Beggar My Neighbour to High-low Draw Poker and from Contract Bridge to Monte Carlo, there is something for every card player, whether young or old, expert or beginner.

Each game is described with step-by-step instructions, complemented by clear, explanatory diagrams; and you will find the answers to those inevitable debates over rules and scoring. As well as tips on strategy and surefire techniques that will turn even the novice player into an expert, there is an easy-to-use, complete glossary of important terms used in card playing.

Contents

SECTION 4. PATIENCE GAMES

Glossary

active player One who is still in the game and has not dropped out or been eliminated.
ante To put up a stake or place a bet before the cards are dealt.
available A card is called available when it fulfils the rules for use in play.
blocked A game that cannot possibly be won.
boodle Cards carrying counters or money chips.
brisque In the game of bezique, a brisque is any ace or 10 contained in a trick.
building Piling cards on top of each other during play in the order prescribed by the particular game. Most often by suit or by colour in numerical order, upwards or downwards.

canasta Name of a game and of a meld of seven cards of the same rank made in that game.
carte blanche A hand containing no court cards.
chips Counters used for placing stakes or bets. In gambling games, chips have a monetary value.
coins Small denominations are often used in social and family games instead of chips.
coming out A game that achieves its aim and is totally resolved.
court cards The K, Q and J of each suit.
cut Dividing a deck of cards into two parts after a shuffle and reversing their positions. The dealing is often determined by cut. Each player cuts the deck and reveals the top card. Depending on the game, the player with the highest card (high cut) or lowest card (low cut) deals. There must be at least five cards in a cut.
dead card or deadwood Cards not used in melds (as in Gin Rummy) or in hands (as in Poker).
deal The way cards are distributed among players at the start of a game.
dealing Laying out the cards before play begins.
deck Pack or set of playing cards used for a game. The standard deck is 52 cards – i.e., four suits of thirteen cards each. Patience games are sometimes played with cards a size smaller than usual if space is at a premium.
deuce The two of each suit.
discard Cards thrown away during play, usually into a discard pile.
discard pile Cards are thrown face up on this pile when they cannot be immediately used to build. They can be brought back into play later, as appropriate.
exposed card Normally only face up, completely

exposed cards are available for play. Cards partly covered are unavailable until fully exposed. Same as upcard.
follow suit Building with a card of the same suit as the previous one on the pile.
foundations Cards on which building takes place.
go knocking Unable to play a card.
hand The cards dealt and the play using those cards.
hole card A card on the table that is unknown to everyone.
layout The arrangement in which the cards are dealt onto the table ready for play.
leader The player to the left of the dealer, who conventionally leads by playing the first card in most card games.
leading suit The suit of the first card played.
meld A group of cards of the same rank or in sequence. Also, to lay out a group of cards or add one or more appropriate cards on an existing meld.
misdeal To deal cards incorrectly.
odd card A single, unpaired card.
odds Chance of winning. Odds of 2 to 1 against, when playing with a bank, mean that out of every three tries, the bank has two chances and the player one chance of winning.
packet A given number of cards conforming to a particular requirement – e.g., a packet may be four cards of the same rank.
pass When a player does not play or bid.
partscore In bridge, a trick score total that is less than the game score total.
patience General name of card games for one player.

piquet deck A deck of 32 cards formed by removing all cards below the 7s from a standard 52-card deck, leaving 7, 8, 9, 10, J, Q, K, ace of each suit.
poker hand Hand of five cards on which players win or lose according to the rank of their hands. There are ten standard hands and two more when wild cards are in use.
pool Same as **pot**.
pot The central collection of stakes. Can literally be a pot to hold chips or coins. Sometimes called the pool.
raise Bet in Poker when a player stakes the same amount as a previous player plus an extra amount. Players usually say 'raise you two' or whatever the amount by which the bet is being raised.
rank Order of cards, or suits, in play. High ranks take precedence over lower ranks.
reserve Cards in the layout that are available for play but are not foundations.
revoke Failure to follow suit.
round the corner The order of cards when joining the ends of a sequence – e.g., Q, K, ace, 2, 3.
sequence A run of cards of the same suit.
setback Penalty for not fulfilling a bid (of tricks).
showdown When everyone shows their hands.
shuffle To mix the cards, by hand. In private games every player has the right to shuffle the cards, but the dealer must make the final shuffle before the deal. In club games only the house dealer shuffles.
slam Winning of all tricks by one player or side.
solitaire Sometimes synonymous with patience but also the name of a board game in its own right.
spaces Gaps in the layout that may or may not be

filled, according to the rules of the game.
stake The number of chips that are being bet.
stand pat Remaining in play but not drawing a card. Sometimes simply called 'stand' or 'stick'.
stock Cards remaining face down in the hand when dealing is complete. They are used in play according to the rules of each game.
stripping Removing certain cards from a standard deck of 52 cards.
suit Clubs, spades, hearts or diamonds.
trey The three of each suit.
trick A group of cards, one from each player in turn according to the rules of the game.
trump A suit that outranks all others. A trump card outranks any card from a plain suit.
upcard Same as **exposed card**.
widow An extra hand dealt to the centre of the table. It usually remains unexposed unless the game allows a player to exchange his or her hand for it.
wild A card that can be used to replace any other card – e.g., joker and 2s are wild cards in canasta.

Bezique

The history of bezique goes back 350 years, the standard game emerging from France. A derivation is pinochle, popular in the USA.

STANDARD BEZIQUE

Players

Standard bezique is for two players, but variations exist for three or four players.

Cards

Bezique is played with a 64-card double piquet deck – i.e. all cards below 7, except the ace, are removed from two standard 52-card decks.

One suit of a piquet deck

The ranking is ace (high), 10, K, Q, J, 9, 8, 7 (low).

Rank for bezique

high low

Aim
Players try to gain the highest points total by making high-scoring tricks and declared melds.

Preparing
Pencil and paper are essential for scoring unless special bezique markers or a cribbage board are available.

Bezique marker

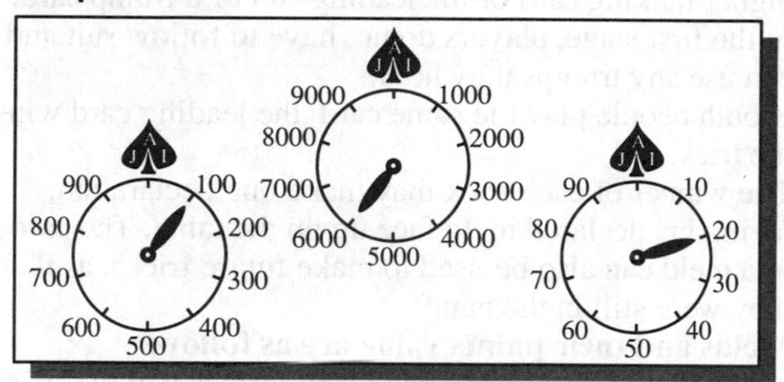

On a cribbage board each hole counts 10

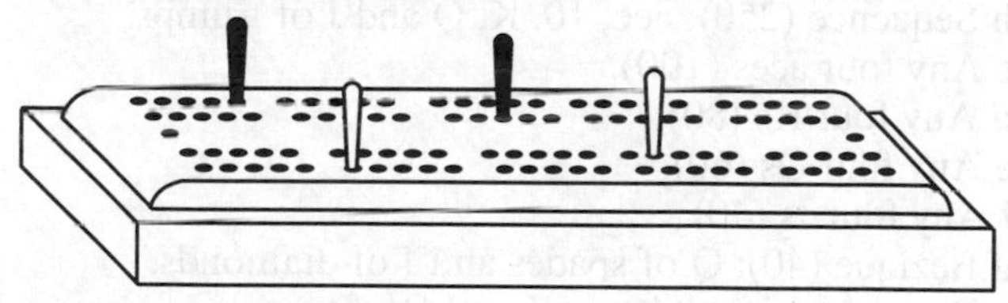

Players agree whether the winning score shall be 1000 points or 2000 points.

Dealing
The dealer is chosen by the higher cut. Packets of three, two and three cards are dealt in three rounds to each player, making a hand of eight cards.
The next card is placed face up to assign trumps. If this

upcard is a 7, the dealer scores 10 points. A stock is made by placing all other cards face down.

Playing: stage one

The non-dealer leads by placing one card face up on the table. The dealer then completes the trick by adding any one of his cards.

The trick is claimed by the player who has placed the higher ranking card of the leading suit or a trump card. In the first stage, players do not have to follow suit and can use any trumps they hold.

If both people play the same card, the leading card wins the trick.

The winner of each trick may make one declaration, laying his declared meld face up on the table. The cards in a meld can also be used to make future tricks, as if they were still in the hand.

Melds and their points value are as follows:

a Double bezique (500): two Qs of spades and two Js of diamonds.

b Sequence (250): ace, 10, K, Q and J of trumps.

c Any four aces (100).

d Any four Ks (80).

e Any four Qs (60).

f Any four Js (40).

g Bezique (40): Q of spades and J of diamonds.

h Royal marriage (40): a K and Q of trumps.

i Common marriage (20): a K and Q of the same non-trump suit.

j Exchange (10): changing the up-card for the 7 of trumps. Whoever holds the other 7 of trumps gains 10 points when he plays it but it is not a declaration.

Cards in melds may be used for later declarations

providing they are not used in similar melds. For example, an ace already used in a four aces declaration cannot be used in a second meld of four aces.

Declarations when clubs are trumps

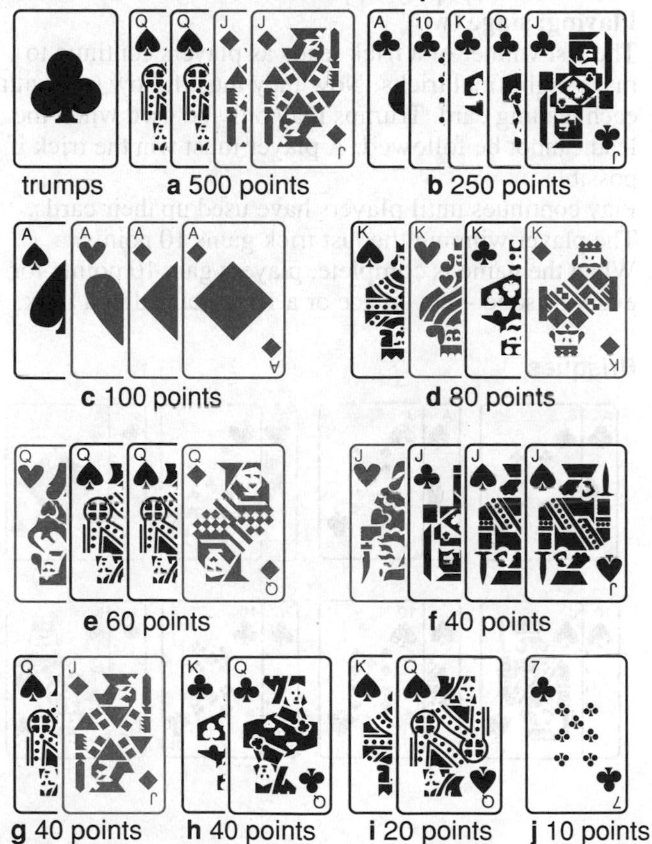

Scores should be recorded as the game proceeds. After the winner has made his declaration he draws cards from the stock to replace those used. The other player then replenishes his hand from the stock. When the stock is used up, players proceed to stage two.

Playing: stage two

The last winner of a trick leads as players continue to make eight final tricks. Now they must follow suit with each leading card. Trumps may only be used when the lead cannot be followed. A player must win the trick if possible.

Play continues until players have used up their cards. The player winning the last trick gains 10 points.

When the game is complete, players gain 10 points for every brisque – i.e. an ace or a 10 contained in a trick.

Brisques

Penalties

1 Opponent scores 10 when a player draws out of turn.
2 Opponent scores 100 when a player holds more than eight cards.
3 A player forfeits 10 of his own points to his opponent when he plays to a trick after he has failed to draw a card during the first stage of play.
4 A player forfeits all eight tricks to his opponent in stage two if he fails to follow suit or take a trick.

Winning the game

The player to first reach 1000 or 2000 points, as agreed, is the winner.

THREE-HANDED BEZIQUE

Three players play for themselves with three piquet decks (96 cards). The final aim is a score of 1500. Otherwise the game is the same as bezique.

RUBICON BEZIQUE

Two people play with four piquet decks (128 cards) and are dealt nine cards singly or in packets of three.
Trumps are assigned by the first sequence or marriage that is declared. Stock cards are not turned up and the 7 of trumps has no value.
Playing proceeds as in standard bezique. The last trick, however, is worth 50 points,and there are four additional types of declaration, as follows:
a Quadruple bezique (4500): four Qs of spades and four Js of diamonds.
b Triple bezique (1500): three Qs of spades and three Js of diamonds.
c Back door or ordinary sequence (150 points): ace, 10, K, Q and J of a non-trump suit.
d Carte blanche (50): declared by a player who has

been dealt a hand without court cards. He displays the carte blanche and draws a card from the stock. Unless this is a court card, he can declare carte blanche again and score a further 50 points. This continues until he draws a court card.

Cards in rubicon melds may be used to make similar

Rubicon declarations when clubs are trumps

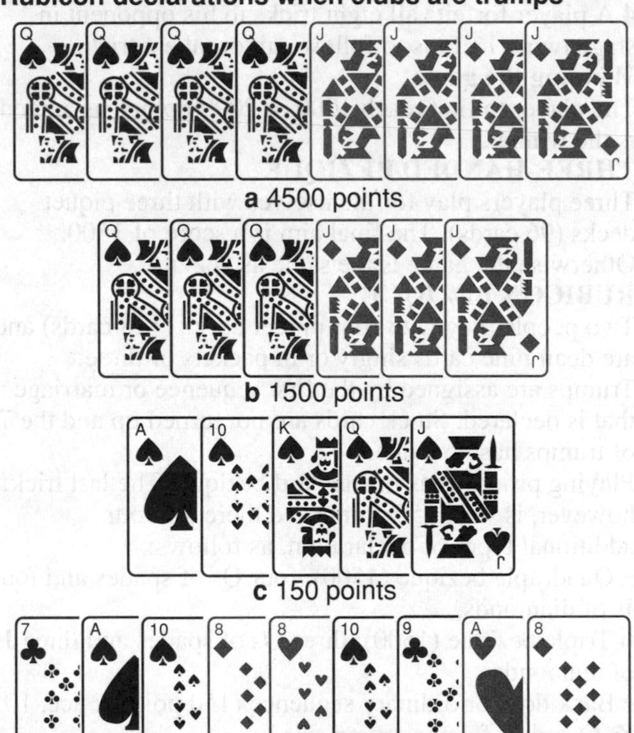

a 4500 points

b 1500 points

c 150 points

d 50 points

combinations. If a Q is played from a meld containing four Qs, for example, another Q can be added to make four Qs again. Also, two more marriages can be made by rearranging two other marriages of the same suit. Brisques are ignored unless there is a tie or a player is about to be rubiconed for failing to make 1000 points. Both players' brisques are then counted.

Winning the game

After one deal, the player with the higher score gains 500 points plus the difference between his own and his opponent's score.

When the loser is rubiconed, his score is nil and the winner gains 1000 points plus 320 for all brisques and the sum of his own and his opponent's score.

If both players have scored less than 1000 points, the one with the higher score is still the winner and gains as above.

The winner gains an extra 100 points if his opponent has scored less than 100 during the game.

If players' scores are close, fractions of 100 points may be taken into account. Otherwise, they are ignored.

SIX-DECK BEZIQUE OR CHINESE BEZIQUE

This game is similar to rubicon bezique but played with six piquet decks (192 cards) and a hand of 12 cards each, dealt singly or in packets of three.

Trumps are assigned by the first declared sequence or marriage. Brisques are never counted. The last, winning trick scores 250 points.

Declarations are as in rubicon bezique, plus five more in the trump suit. Also, carte blanche scores 250. Six-deck declarations (in trumps) and their points value are (overleaf):

a four aces (1000)
b four 10s (900)
c four Ks (800)
d four Qs (600)
e four Js (400)

Six-deck declarations when spades are trumps

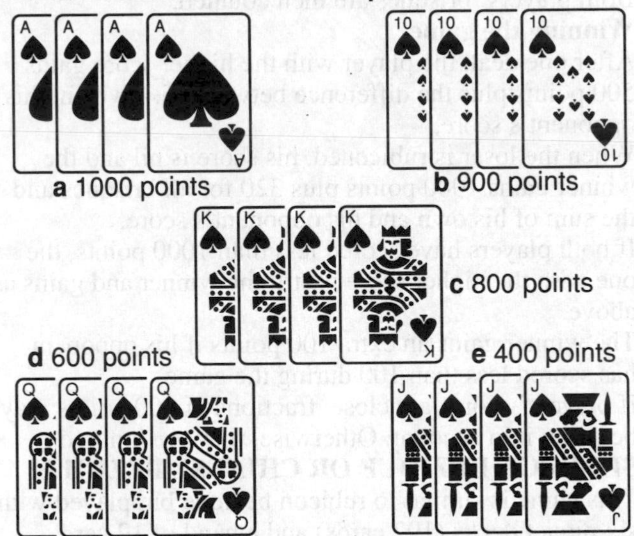

A bezique is declared according to the trump suit

trumps hearts — trumps diamonds — trumps clubs — trumps spades

Winning the game

Scores are made after a single game as for rubicon except the winner's bonus is 1000 points and a player is rubiconed for a score less than 3000, not 1000.

EIGHT-DECK BEZIQUE

Played as six-deck but with eight piquet decks (256

Eight-deck declarations when clubs are trumps

a 9000 points
b 2000 points
c 1800 points
d 1600 points
e 1200 points
f 800 points
g 50 points

cards) and a hand of 15 cards each. Declarations are similar to six-deck declarations with differences (and points values) as listed:

a Quintuple bezique (9000)
b Five trump aces (2000)
c Five trump 10s (1800)
d Five trump Ks (1600)
e Five trump Qs (1200)
f Five trump Js (800)
g Bezique (50)

With a score less than 5000 a player is rubiconed.

FOUR-HANDED BEZIQUE

Similar to rubicon bezique but played with six piquet decks (192 cards) and each player is dealt nine cards. Players pair up, with partners sitting opposite each other.

Four-handed declarations with diamonds as trumps

a 40,500 points

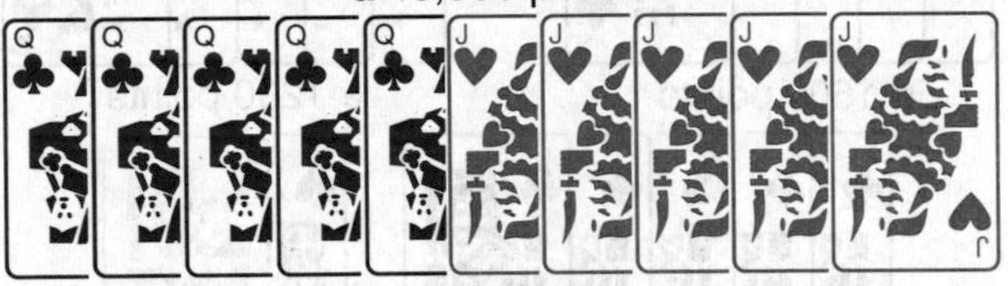

b 13,500 points

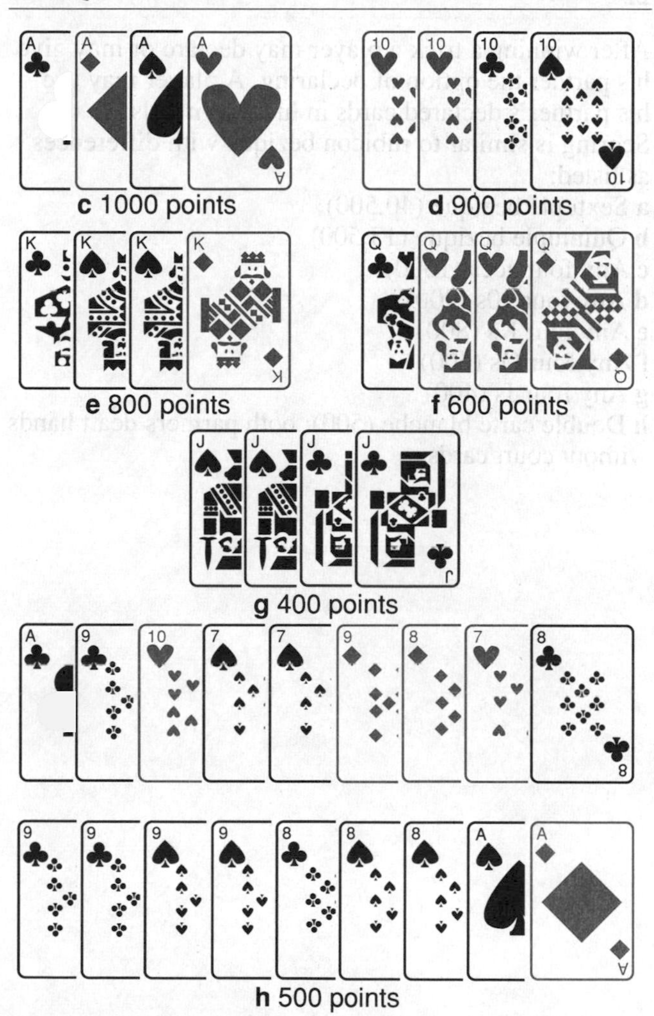

c 1000 points

d 900 points

e 800 points

f 600 points

g 400 points

h 500 points

After winning a trick a player may declare or may give his partner the option of declaring. A player may use his partner's declared cards in his own melds.

Scoring is similar to rubicon bezique with differences as listed:

a Sextuple bezique (40,500)
b Quintuple bezique (13,500)
c Any four aces (1000)
d Any four 10s (900)
e Any four Ks (800)
f Any four Qs (600)
g Any four Js (400)
h Double carte blanche (500): both partners dealt hands without court cards.

Boston

A variation of whist which was popular during the American Revolution.

Players

Four people play individually. Sitting positions can be agreed by cutting the deck, each person choosing their place in order.

Cards

Two standard 52-card decks are required. The one not used in play is used to select the rank order of suits known as preference, colour and plain. Ace ranks high. A trick is a set of four cards, one played in turn by each person.

Rank

Aim

Players score by making and fulfilling bids.

Preparing

A number of chips are needed for scoring. Each person begins with the same number. (Some authorities recommend 1000 each in fives, tens, twenties and fifties, to make settlement easier.) Before the first deal, each player puts 10 chips into the pool. If the pool contains more than 250, excess chips are put aside and added to the next pool.

Dealing
The first dealer is chosen by high cut, ace ranking low. The whole of one pack is shuffled and dealt clockwise in four packets of three followed by a single card to each player. The dealer forfeits 10 of his chips to the pool if he misdeals, and the deal passes to the player on his left.

Ranking the suits
The second deck of cards can then be shuffled by anyone before being cut in half by the player opposite to the dealer. He then turns up the top card of the bottom half, which assigns the preference suit. The suit of the same colour is called the colour suit and the other two are plain suits.

Cutting for preference

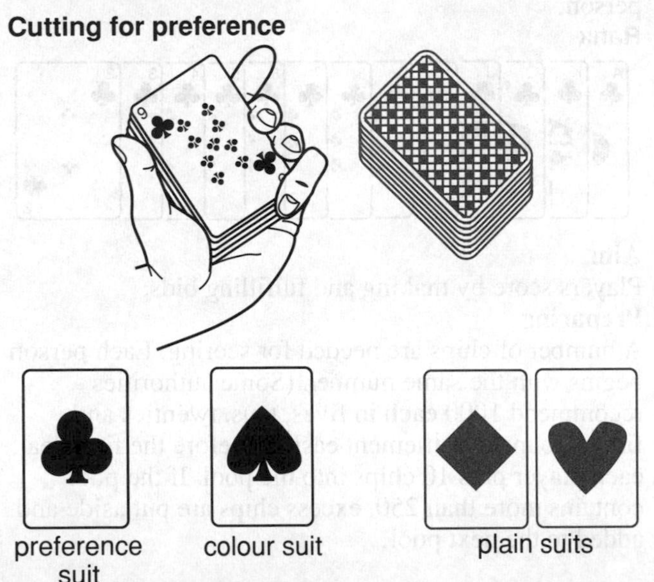

Bidding
The player to the dealer's left begins by passing or bidding. Each player makes a bid in turn, clockwise. Except for no trump bids, a player chooses his own trumps but usually waits until his bid is accepted before declaring it.
The bids have a rank order from **a** (low) to **m** (high), each onc outbidding those above it, as follows:
a Boston: make five tricks declaring one of the plain suits as trumps.
b Make six tricks.
c Make seven tricks.
d Little misery: lose 12 tricks, with no trumps. Before play each person discards one card face down.
e Make eight tricks.
f Make nine tricks.
g Grand misery: lose all 13 tricks with no trumps.
h Make 10 tricks.
i Make 11 tricks.
j Little spread: lose 12 tricks, with no trumps and the hand of cards face up on the table.
k Make 12 tricks.
l Grand spread: losc all 13 tricks, with no trumps and the hand of cards face up on the table.
m Grand slam: make all 13 tricks.
If two or more players bid to make the same number of tricks, the trump suit they each choose is ranked preference suit (high), colour suit and plain suit (low), thus ranking their bids.
Passing
If all four players pass, everyone discards their hands

and adds 10 chips to the pool. A new shuffle and deal is made by the person to the dealer's left.

Playing

The player who made the highest bid aims to fulfil his bid, while the other players attempt to prevent him.
The player to the left of the dealer leads by laying a card face up on the table. The others must follow suit if possible and may only trump or play another suit if they have no cards in the leading suit.

Revoking

A player who fails to follow suit is said to revoke.
Anyone who revokes must pay 40 chips into the pool and lose his hand.

Settlement

When all 13 tricks have been made, accounts are settled.

1 The player who fulfils his bid is paid by each of the other players. If his bid was for seven or more tricks, he also gets the pool.

2 The player who fails to make his bid number of tricks pays the other players. He must also double the number of chips in the pool.

Fulfilled bids to make tricks are paid according to table **A.**

Failed bids to make tricks must pay according to table **B.**

The number of tricks by which a player fails to fulfil his bid are called the 'number put in for'.

Bids to lose tricks pay or are paid according to table **C.**
The one who fails pays all players, or all players pay the one who fulfils his bid.

Table A

tricks bid	5	6	7	8	9	10	11	12	13
payment	10	15	20	25	35	45	70	120	180

Table B

number put in for	tricks bid								
	5	6	7	8	9	10	11	12	13
	payment								
1	10	15	20	25	35	45	70	120	180
2	20	25	30	35	45	55	80	130	200
3	30	35	40	45	55	70	95	145	220
4	40	45	50	55	65	80	110	160	240
5	50	55	60	70	80	95	125	180	260
6		65	70	85	95	110	140	200	280
7			80	100	110	125	155	220	300
8				115	125	140	170	240	320
9					140	155	185	260	340
10						170	200	280	360
11							220	300	390
12								320	420
13									450

Table C

bid	payment
little misery	20
grand misery	40
little spread	80
grand spread	160

Bridge

Bridge emerged in 1896, a development from the older game of whist. Auction bridge evolved in 1904, and in 1925, contract bridge was formulated and soon became the most popular form of bridge.

CONTRACT BRIDGE

Players

Four people play in pairs. Partners sit opposite to each other and are called north-south and east-west respectively.

Cards

The game calls for the standard deck of 52 cards. Ace ranks high. The 2 is known as deuce and the 3 trey.
A second deck with different backs is often shuffled while the deal takes place, in preparation for the next deal.
A set of four cards, one played in turn by each person, is called a trick.
During the bidding, suits are ranked spades (high), hearts, diamonds and clubs (low).
Honours are the four aces when there are no trumps. When there are trumps, honours are the ace, K, Q, J and 10 of trumps.

Rank

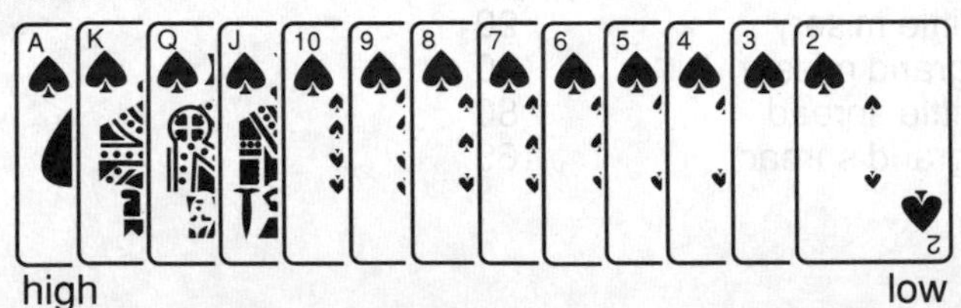

no trump honours

    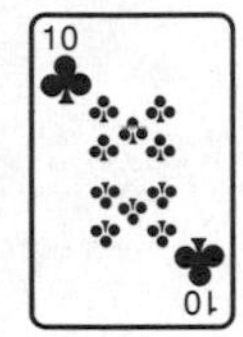

honours when clubs are trumps

Rank of suits

high low

Aim

A partnership aims to win the most points in the best of three games, known as a rubber.

Preparing

One deck is spread face down, from which each player draws one card. Those with the two highest cards become partners, as do the two who draw the two lowest cards.

The player holding the highest card becomes the dealer and chooses where to sit, with his partner sitting opposite. If cards of the same value are drawn, they are ranked by suit.

Any player can shuffle the cards before the dealer makes the final shuffle and invites the player on his left to cut. Meanwhile, the dealer's partner shuffles the second deck.
Bridge score pads and pencils are required.

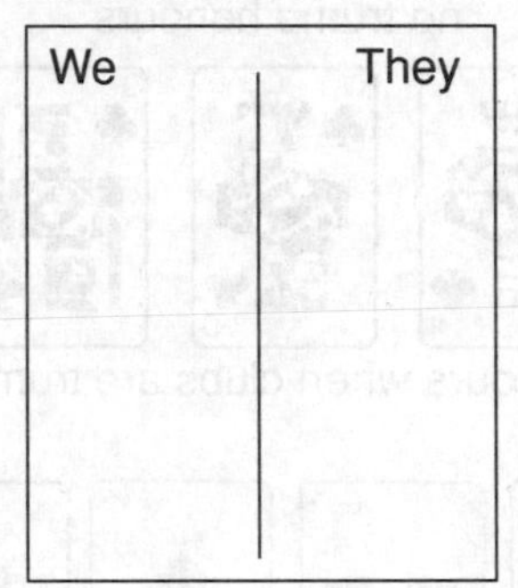

Scoring pad for contract bridge

Dealing
Beginning with the player on the dealer's left, the cards are dealt singly, face down in clockwise rotation, until each player has 13 cards.
Bidding
When everyone has examined the cards in their hands the auction is begun by the dealer. The other players call in turn in clockwise rotation.
A player can call bid, pass, double or redouble:
a A pass means a player does not wish to bid; he can make another call later. If all four players pass in the first round of the auction, all cards are thrown in and the person to the left of the dealer shuffles and deals again. When three passes follow a bid, double or redouble, the auction ends.
b A player who bids calls the number of tricks in excess

of six that his partnership will make in a stated trump suit or in no trumps. For example, calls of 'two clubs' or 'five no trumps' means the player believes his partnership can make eight tricks with clubs as trumps, or 11 tricks with no trumps.
Each bid must be higher than the one before it by the player calling a larger number of tricks or a higher ranking trump suit. 'No trumps' ranks highest of all. The rank order of some sample bids would be:

1 seven no trumps (highest possible call; known as a grand slam)
2 six no trumps (known as a small slam)
3 five diamonds
4 four no trumps
5 four spades
6 four hearts
7 four diamonds
8 four clubs
9 three clubs
10 one clubs (lowest possible call)

c A player calls double when he believes he could prevent the previous bid from being made if it became the contract. The bid can be outbid by any player as normal, in which case it does not become the contract. However, if a doubled bid does become the contract, the scores are doubled by the winners if they fulfil their contract or by the partnership that called double if the contract is not fulfilled.

d When their bid has been doubled, one of the bidding partnership may call redouble, reasserting their confidence in their bid. A bid that has been redoubled can be outbid by either partnership.

The contract
The partnership from which the highest call came in the auction now has to fulfil that contract during play. Their opponents aim to prevent them.

The declarer
The member of the contracting partnership who first bid no trumps or a trump suit (spades, hearts, diamonds, clubs), is called the declarer and plays both hands. His partner, called the dummy, lays his hand on the table when the lead card has been played. He takes no further part in the play of that deal.

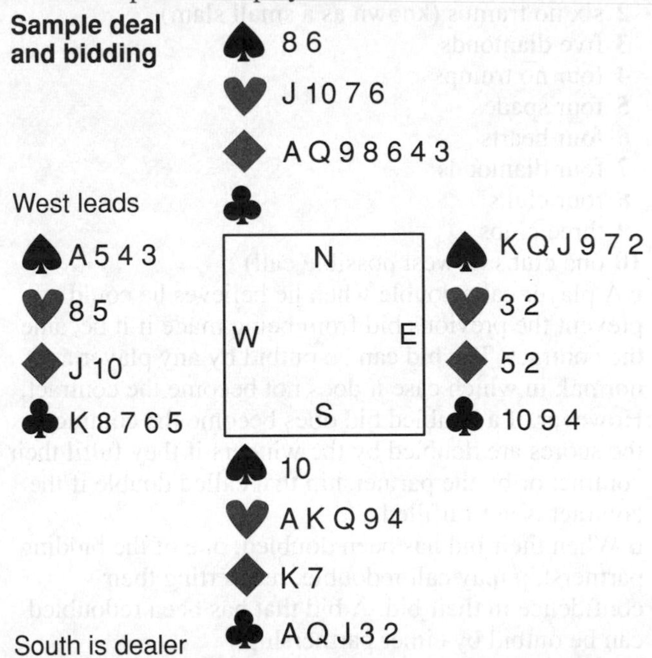

Bidding

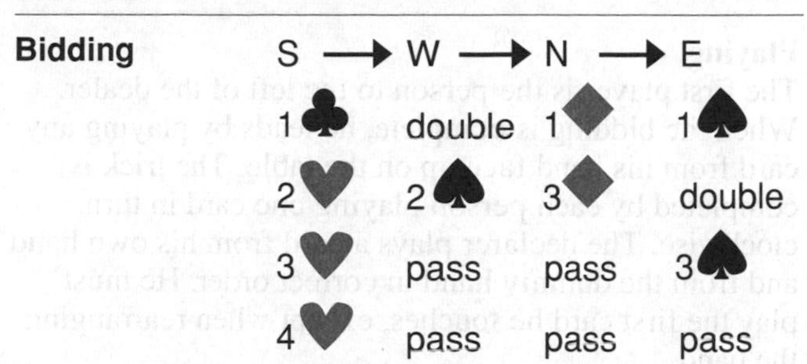

The contract is four hearts to be made by North-South. South is the declarer. North and his hand are the dummy. His cards are placed face up on the table, trumps to his right and other suits ranked in rows.

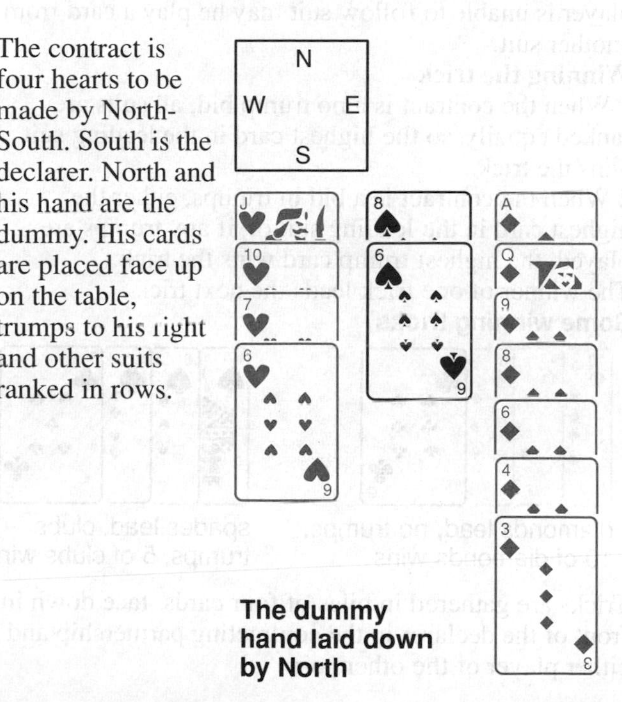

The dummy hand laid down by North

Playing

The first player is the person to the left of the dealer. When the bidding is complete, he leads by playing any card from his hand face up on the table. The trick is completed by each person playing one card in turn, clockwise. The declarer plays a card from his own hand and from the dummy hand in correct order. He must play the first card he touches, except when rearranging the hand.

Every card must follow the leading suit. Only if a player is unable to follow suit may he play a card from another suit.

Winning the trick

1 When the contract is a no trump bid, all suits are ranked equally, so the highest card in the leading suit wins the trick.

2 When the contract is a bid in trumps, either the highest card in the leading suit or, if any trumps are played, the highest trump card wins the trick.

The winner of one trick leads the next trick.

Some winning tricks

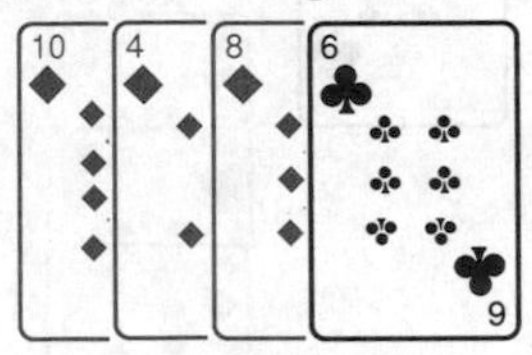

diamonds lead, no trumps, 10 of diamonds wins

spades lead, clubs trumps, 5 of clubs wins

Tricks are gathered in piles of four cards, face down in front of the declarer in the contracting partnership and either player of the other pair.

Tricks are piled to show how many have been made. Any trick can be inspected before the inspecting partnership plays in the next trick.

Fulfilling the contract

The contracting partnership is said to have 'made the book' when their first six tricks are taken. They must then make at least the number of tricks they bid. The tricks in the book are piled together so that the extra tricks can be clearly counted.

Scoring

Both partnerships should keep scores to avoid disputes. Scores also affect the strategy of the game. A horizontal line is drawn across the WE (one partnership) and the THEY (the opponents) columns. Points can be scored 'below the line' and 'above the line'.

1 Below the line (trick points): Only the declarer's partnership scores trick points if they have fufilled the contract for the hand. Only the extra tricks are scored below the line.
2 Above the line (premium points): Both sides score premium points if they achieve any of the following in the hand:
overtricks (tricks over the number bid);
doubling or redoubling successfully;
making a slam that was bid;
honour cards dealt in the hand;
winning the final game of a rubber; or
undertricks, which the declarer's partnership fails to make to complete their contract. Their value is added to the opponent's score.
A partnership is said to be vulnerable when its first game towards a rubber has been won. When the score is one game all, both partnerships are vulnerable.

Winning the game

Progress towards winning a game is shown by the number of trick points; 100 or more wins a game. More than one hand may be played.
After each hand, a horizontal line is drawn below the trick scores of both partnerships. Scoring tricks for the next game begins from zero, below this line. Premium scores continue above the line without division.

Winning the rubber

The first side to win two games scores 700 premium points if the opponents have not won a game, 500 if they have. The rubber is won by the partnership with the higher total of combined trick and premium points.

Back scoring
In a competition where partners rotate, the status of an individual is calculated by back scoring after each rubber:

1 the losing partnership's score is deducted from the winner's to find the difference;
2 the difference is rounded up to the nearest 100 – for example, 750 becomes 800;
3 the rounded difference is divided by 100 – for example, 800 becomes eight; and
4 the winning partners are given a plus score for the rubber (for example, plus eight). The losers get the same minus score (minus eight).

Winning the competition
As individuals play further rubbers with different partners, they acquire plus or minus scores. At the end of the competition, the player with the highest plus score is the overall winner.

Recording scores on the scoring pad

a

We	They
70	

b

We	They
150	
70	
30	

a WE score 70 trick points.
b WE score 30 trick points and 150 premium points.

WE win the first game (100 trick points) and a line is drawn across both columns. WE are now vulnerable.

c

We	They
150	200
70	
30	

d

We	They
	150
150	200
70	
30	
	60

c WE fail to make a contract by two tricks. THEY score 200 vulnerable undertrick points.
d THEY score 60 trick points and 150 premium points.

Scoring table for contract bridge

Declarer's below-the-line trick scores	**♣**	**♦**	**♥**	**♠**	**NT**
first extra trick (over six) bid and made	20	20	30	30	40
subsequent tricks bid and made	20	20	30	30	30
doubling (double the trick score)	40	40	60	60	80
redoubling (double the doubled score)	80	80	120	120	140

Above-the-line scores	**not vulnerable**	**vulnerable**
small slam	500	750
grand slam	1000	1500
undoubled overtrick	Trick value	Trick value
doubled overtrick	100	200
redoubled overtrick	200	400
fulfilling a doubled	50	50
redoubled contract	100	100

Rubber, game and partscore	**points**
winning rubber (opponents have no game)	700
winning rubber (opponents have one game)	500
winning one game in unfinished rubber	300
having the only partscore in unfinished rubber	50

Honours (in one hand)	**points**
four trump honours	100
five trump honours	150
four aces (no trump contract)	150

Undertricks	**a**	**b**	**c**
first trick (not vulnerable)	50	100	200
next two tricks	50	200	400
subsequent tricks	50	300	600
first trick (vulnerable)	100	200	400
subsequent tricks	100	300	600

a = undoubled
b = doubled
c = redoubled

DUPLICATE CONTRACT BRIDGE

An advanced form of bridge – the only one played in international tournaments – in which several groups of players, in turn, receive the same deal of cards, thus testing skill rather than luck.

AUCTION BRIDGE

Auction bridge lies between whist and contract bridge in the evolution of the game. The rules are the same as for contract bridge, but the scoring is different, which affects the players' strategy.

The main differences in the method of scoring are:

1 Vulnerability does not exist, so there is no extra penalty for failing to fulfil a contract when one partnership has already won a game.

2 Odd tricks – i.e., more than the book of six – are scored below the line whether or not they were contracted for and count toward winning the game if the declarer has at least fulfilled the contract.

	♣	♦	♥	♠	NT
Scoring trick points					
undoubled	6	7	8	9	10
doubled	12	14	16	18	20
redoubled	24	28	32	36	40

Winning the game
The partnership that first scores 30 points below the line wins that game, and a line is drawn across the score pad, as in contract bridge.
Winning the rubber
The first partnership to win two games wins that rubber and gains 250 extra points.
Scoring conventions
Three or more honours in the trump suit, or three or more aces in no trumps, earn points (scored above the line) for the partnership that holds them, whichever partnership it is. The honours score as follows:

Three honours (or aces):	30 points
Four honours (or aces) divided:	40
Five honours divided:	50
Four honours in one hand:	80
Five honours divided four to one:	90
Four aces in one hand:	100
Five honours in one hand:	100

If a partnership bids and fulfils a doubled contract, the declarer scores 50 bonus points above the line and 50

points for every trick above the contracted number.
If a redoubled contract is bid and made, declarer's side gains 100 bonus points and 100 points for each trick exceeding the contract.
The opponents acquire points above the line for each trick the declarer's partnership fails to make (undertrick), as follows:

Undoubled contract:	50
Doubled contract:	100
Redoubled contract:	200

Whatever the contract bid, a small slam (12 tricks), made by either side, scores 50 points above the line and a grand slam (13 tricks) scores 100 points.

Canasta

A game from the rummy family, canasta was developed in Uruguay and passed via Argentina to the USA in 1949, where its popularity peaked in the 1950s.

Players

Four people play and score in pairs. Two or three people can also play individually.

Cards

The canasta deck of 108 cards consists of any two standard decks of 52, plus four jokers. Cards are not ranked but have points values (see table).

Table of points values of cards

card by denomination	points value and name
red 3 (diamond and heart)	100 bonus card
	800 (if a pair hold four)
joker	50 wild card
deuce (2)	20 wild card
ace	20 natural card
8, 9, 10, J, Q, K	10 natural cards
4, 5, 6, 7	5 natural cards
black 3 (club and spade)	5 stop card

Melds

Three or more cards make a meld, which must contain:
1 only cards of the same denomination;
2 at least two natural cards;
3 not more than three wild cards;
4 no red 3s; and
5 no black 3s unless the player is going out.
A meld of seven cards is called a canasta, which can be natural or mixed and attracts bonus points.

Examples of some melds

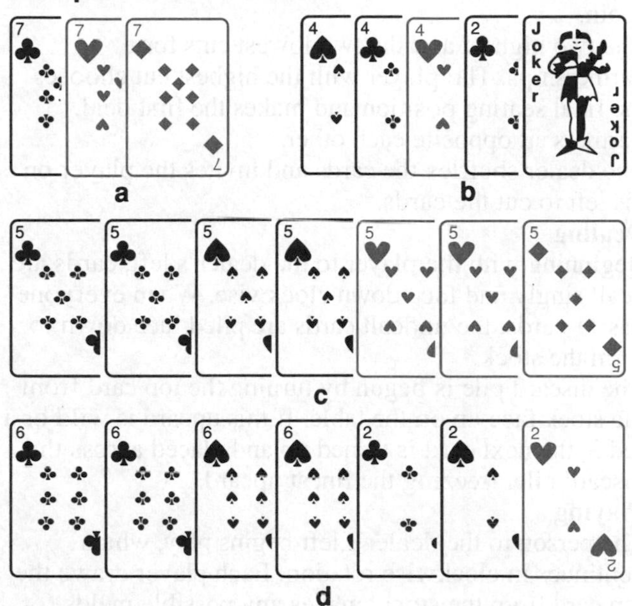

a three natural cards
b three natural and two wild cards
c a natural canasta of seven natural cards
d a mixed canasta of four natural and three wild cards

Aim

To be the first pair to gain 5000 points.

Preparing

Paper and pencil are needed for scoring. A score-keeper is chosen by consensus, or a non-player may take the job. All players cut the canasta deck, the cards ranking normally with ace high and suits ranking spades high, hearts, diamonds and clubs. Anyone cutting a joker cuts again.

The two highest and the two lowest cuts form partnerships. The player with the highest cut chooses the final seating position and makes the first deal. Partners sit opposite each other.

The dealer shuffles the cards and invites the player on his left to cut the cards.

Dealing

Beginning with the player to the dealer's left, cards are dealt singly and face down clockwise. When everyone has 11 cards, the undealt cards are piled face down to form the stock.

The discard pile is begun by turning the top card from the stock face up on the table. If this upcard is wild or a red 3, the next card is turned up and placed across the discard pile, freezing the finest upcard.

Playing

The person to the dealer's left begins play, which continues in clockwise rotation. Each player draws the top card from the stock, makes any possible melds (or adds to those of his partner) and finally places a card in the discard pile. The procedure is as follows:

1 Any red 3s held in the hand must be laid out face up and replaced with cards from the stock.

2 The first meld of the deal must reach a value fixed by the partnerships' accumulated score (see table).

3 Any canasta melded is gathered into a pile. A red card is put on top of a natural canasta and a black card on top of a mixed one.

4 More cards may be added to the partnership's existing canastas except that a fourth wild card cannot be added to a mixed canasta and no wild card can be added to a natural canasta.

Table A

accumulated score from previous deals	minimum value of first meld of next deal
3000 upwards	120
1500 to 2995	90
0 to 1495	50
minus score	15

The discard

If it is not frozen, the discard pile can be acquired as follows:

1 A player of a partnership that has already laid out melds may take the upcard instead of one from the stock if his hand contains at least two natural cards of the same value as the upcard.

2 The upcard must then be melded by adding it to two natural cards or to one of the partnership's existing melds.

(It is generally accepted that the upcard cannot be added to a canasta. Also, the old ruling allowed it to be added to a natural and a wild card, but this is not usual in modern play.)

3 The whole of the discard pile may then be taken into the player's hand.

4 As many cards as possible are then used from the hand to add to melds or make new ones. Any red 3 picked up in the discard must be laid out.

5 One card is finally thrown away, as in basic play.

If the stock pile runs out, the remaining discard pile is turned face down to use as stock.

A discard pile is frozen and cannot be picked up:

a by a partnership that has not made the first meld of the deal;
b by a player whose turn it is when the upcard is a black 3 (the pile is unfrozen when he throws his discard on it); or
c by any player when the upcard is a wild card or red 3.
All discards are then put across the pile until someone unfreezes it by melding a subsequent upcard card with two natural cards.

The frozen discard

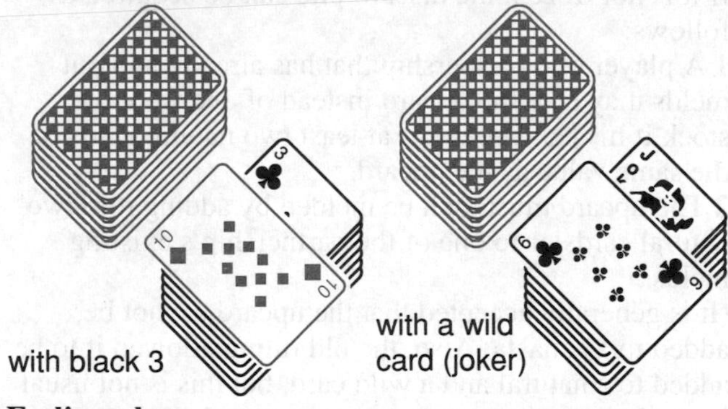

Ending play
A player wanting to go out at his next turn usually asks 'may I go out partner?' so his partner can take appropriate action. The reply may be yes or no, and must be obeyed.
Any player can go out by melding all his cards, providing he lays down a canasta or his partnership has already made one. Three or four black 3s may be melded together only to go out and may not be melded with wild cards.

Going out concealed happens when a player has not melded any cards on the table before his final turn.

Scoring

In addition to the denomination value of the cards, bonus points and penalty points are allotted.

One to three red 3s:	+100 each
Four red 3s:	+800
Going out:	+100
Going out concealed:	+200
Natural canasta:	+500
Mixed canasta:	+300

If a partnership has not made a first meld, there are penalties for holding red 3s, as follows:

Holding one to three red 3s:	-100 each
Holding four red 3s:	-800
Failing to reveal a red 3:	-200

Recording the scores

Each partnership should have a plus and a minus column on the score sheet.

A partnership's plus column should include:
1 total value of cards in melds;
2 bonus for going out;
3 bonus for mixed canastas;
4 bonus for natural canastas; and
5 bonus for red 3s.

A partnership's minus column should include:
1 total value of cards still held at end of play; and
2 any penalty points.

The total of minus points is deducted from the plus total to give the partnership's score.

Winning the game
Hands are played until one partnership reaches 5000 points.

CANASTA VARIATIONS

Canasta is adaptable for any number of players from two to six. It is an exciting game of strategy; the variations selected here offer many strategic alternatives. They are played to standard canasta rules with modifications as described for each variation.

TWO-HANDED CANASTA

Each player is dealt 15 cards. During play two cards are drawn from the stock and one is discarded. Two canastas must be melded before going out.

CUTTHROAT CANASTA

This is the standard game played by only three people, each playing for himself with a hand of 11 cards. The following modifications to the standard rules are optional.

Playing
At each turn, two cards are drawn from the stock and one discarded. Each person plays for himself until one person takes the discard pile. This player then continues to play alone, and the other two join forces in partnership against him.
When a player goes out without anyone having taken the discard, he scores as the lone player against the partnership of the other two.
If the stock is exhausted before anyone goes out, play ends after the player who drew the last stock card has discarded.
The value of a starting meld may be different for each partner, according to his accumulated score.

Cutthroat partnership

Scoring

Red 3s count for individual players; otherwise the partnership score is credited to both partners. The game is won by the player who first reaches a score of 7500 points.

FIVE-HANDED CANASTA

Played in partnerships exactly as standard four-handed canasta. One side has three players, who take turns to sit out at each deal.

SIX-HANDED CANASTA

There are either two partnerships of three players seated A B A B A B, or three partnerships of two seated A B C A B C.

Six-handed partnerships

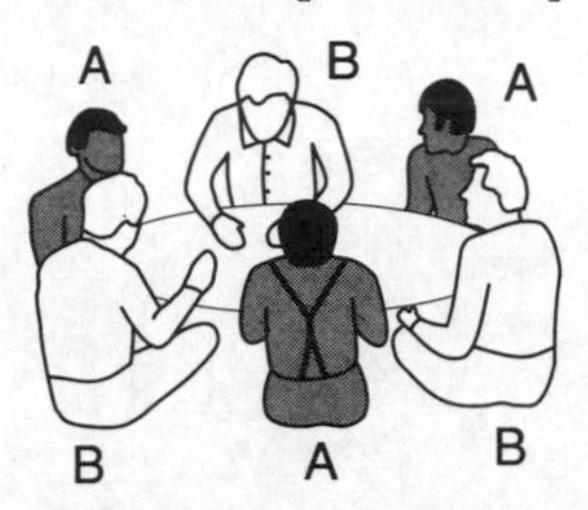

partnership A plays against partnership B

A, B and C partnerships play against each other

A deck of 162 cards is used – i.e., 3 x 52 plus 6 jokers.
Each player is dealt 13 cards.
A score of 10,000 wins the game.
When a partnership's score reaches 7000, its initial meld must be worth 150 points.
Up to four red 3s count 100 points each. Five red 3s count 1000, and all six red 3s count 1200.
To go out, two canastas must have been melded by the partnership.

BOLIVIAN CANASTA

A partnership game for four people, played as standard canasta with the following differences.

Cards

A deck of 162 cards is used – i.e., 3 x 52 plus 6 jokers.
Each player is dealt 15 cards. Two cards are drawn from the stock at each turn and one discarded.

Aim

To win the game by scoring 15,000 points.

Accumulated scores from previous deals	Minimum value of first meld of next deal
minus score	15 points
0 to 1495	50 points
1500 to 2995	90 points
3000 to 6995	120 points
7000 or more	150 points

Wild cards

From three to seven wild cards (deuces and jokers) can be used to make a meld. A canasta of wild cards (seven cards) is called a Bolivia.

A Bolivia

2500 points

Sequence melds

Three or more cards forming a run of the same suit can be used to make a sequence meld. Suits rank from ace (high) to 4 (low); 3s and deuces cannot be included. Sequence melds can be natural or mixed with wild cards and score as normal. An Escalera is a natural sequence canasta (a run of seven cards of the same suit with no wild cards).

Mixed sequence canasta 300 points

An Escalera 1500 points

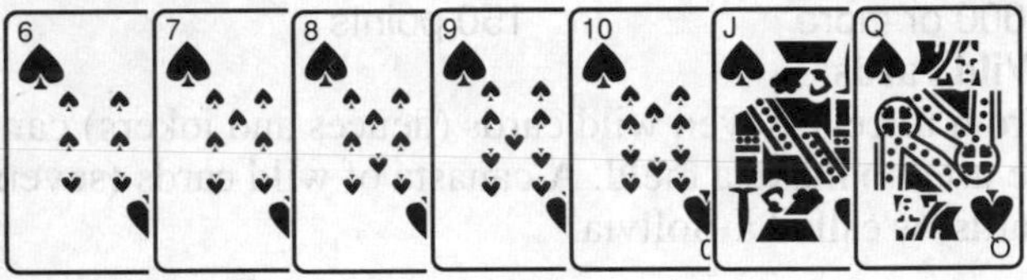

Going out
Two canastas are required to go out, one of which must be an Escalera.

Additional scoring
A Bolivia (wild canasta) scores 2500 points.
An Escalera (natural sequence canasta) scores 1500 points.
Red 3s count 100 points; all six score 1000.
Red 3 scores are plus when any two canastas have been made. If not, red 3 scores are minus.
Black 3s in melds count 5 points but left in the hand they count minus 100 points.

PENNIES FROM HEAVEN
Six people play in two partnerships of three, with a deck of 216 cards – i.e., 4 x 52 plus 8 jokers. Players sit in order A B A B A B around the table.

Dealing
Each player is dealt 13 cards singly, and finally a packet of 11 cards which remain face down until the player has made the first canasta. He may then choose to add the packet of 11 cards to his hand.

A sample hand dealt for Pennies from Heaven

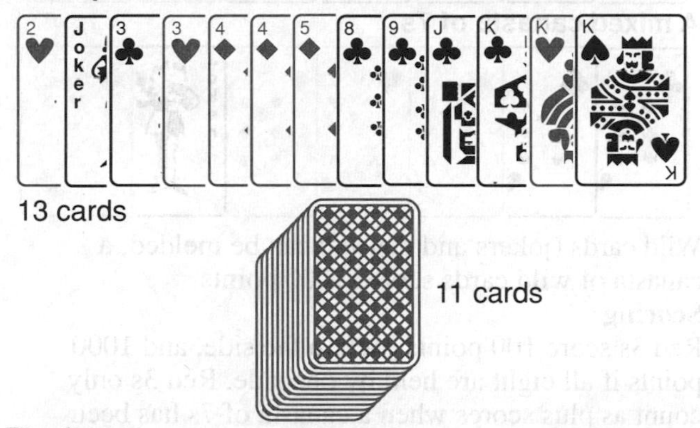

Playing
Two cards are taken from the stock and one discarded at each turn. Canastas may not include more than seven cards.
If a player wants to go out, his side must have made four canastas: one natural, one mixed, one wild and one of 7s.
The discard may not be a 7 until both sides have melded a canasta of 7s, whether mixed or natural; both types score 1500 points. A 7 may not be used when discarding to go out.

A natural canasta of 7s

A mixed canasta of 7s

Wild cards (jokers and deuces) can be melded; a canasta of wild cards scores 1000 points.

Scoring

Red 3s score 100 points each to the side, and 1000 points if all eight are held by one side. Red 3s only count as plus scores when a canasta of 7s has been made; otherwise they count minus.

Accumulated scores from previous deals	Minimum value of first meld of next deal
Minus	15 points
0 to 495	50 points
500 to 995	90 points
1000 to 1495	120 points
1500 or more	150 points

The game is won by the side first reaching a score of 20,000 points.

MEXICANA

A partnership game for four players. A triple deck of 162 cards is used – i.e., 3 x 52 plus 6 jokers. Everyone is dealt 13 cards.

Playing

The player who makes the starting meld for his side draws 13 cards from the top of the stock to add to his hand.

When a 7 is on top, the discard pile cannot be taken. Sevens are melded as in standard canasta, but both mixed and natural canastas of 7s score 1000 points.

Going out

A partnership going out must have made two canastas and hold as many red 3s as it has made canastas.

Red 3s to go out in Mexicana

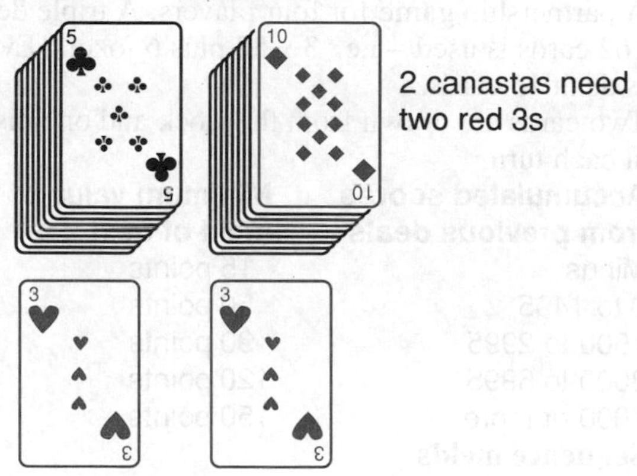

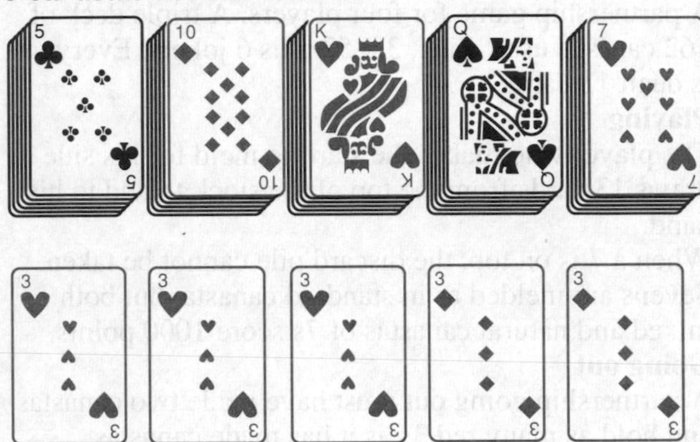

SAMBA

A partnership game for four players. A triple deck of 162 cards is used – i.e., 3 x 52 plus 6 jokers. Everyone is dealt 15 cards.

Two cards are drawn from the stock and one discarded at each turn.

Accumulated scores from previous deals	Minimum value of first meld of next deal
Minus	15 points
0 to 1495	50 points
1500 to 2995	90 points
3000 to 6995	120 points
7000 or more	150 points

Sequence melds

Sequence melds and canastas may be made by using three to seven cards of the same suit, running in rank order sequence (ace high to 4 low). A sequence canasta (seven cards) is called a samba and scores 1500 points.

No wild cards may be used and no further cards can be added to a samba.

Normal melds

No more than two wild cards may be used to make a mixed canasta.

Partnerships can combine their melds to make canastas or sambas.

The discard pile

The top card of the discard may not be added to a completed canasta, only to a meld of fewer than seven cards. The discard pile may only be taken by melding its top card with a natural pair from the hand.

Going out

To go out a partnership must have two canastas, two sambas or one of each.

Red 3s are only counted by the partnership going out: 100 each and 1000 for holding all six.

The bonus for going out is 200 points, but there is no extra bonus for going out concealed.

Winning the game

The winning side is credited the difference between their opponent's score and their own. Scores should therefore be checked after each deal to see if the difference would take one partnership up to the winning score of 10,000 points.

Calculating the scores

partnership A score:	5600 points
partnership B score:	3400 points
difference:	2200
add higher score:	5600
total:	7800 (insufficient to win game)

Later in the game:

partnership A score:	6950 points
partnership B score:	3810 points
difference:	3140
add higher score:	6950
total:	10,090 points (partnership A wins the game)

COMBO-CANASTA

A high-scoring partnership game for four players. A triple deck of 162 cards is used – i.e., 3 x 52 plus 6 jokers. Everyone is dealt 15 cards.

Playing

Two cards are taken from the stock pile and one discarded. The discard pile is always frozen, so may only be taken if two natural cards are held that match the upcard.

In each deal, the first player to make a canasta gets a bonus of 11 cards from the stock.

There is no going out. The play for a deal ends when the stock is exhausted and any remaining discard is refused.

A game consists of four deals.

Accumulated scores from previous deals	Minimum value of first meld of next deal
0 to 3495	60 points
3500 to 6995	100 points
7000 to 10,495	140 points
10,500 and over	180 points

Melds and canastas

Only two wild cards can be used in mixed canastas. Wild cards may be melded by themselves in sequences of three or more runs. Canastas score as shown in the table.

Table of canasta scores

Bolivia (wild cards)	2000
Escalera (sequence)	1500
Samba (natural 7s)	1500
Mixed 7s	1000
Red canasta (natural)	500
Black canasta (mixed)	300

Red 3s score positive if the partnership has made a Bolivia, an Escalera or a Samba. If not, red 3s count as minus scores.

Scoring

At the end of four deals, each partnership deducts the value of cards left in the hand from the value of melds, canastas and red 3s, providing the required canastas have been made. The partnership with the higher score wins the game.

Points value of individual cards

cards	value	penalty value
jokers	50	-50
deuces	20	-20
aces	20	-20
K, Q, J, 10, 9, 8	10	-10
6,5,4	5	-5
7s	5	-500
black 3s	5	-200
red 3s	100	-100
six red 3s	2000	-2000
undeclared red 3		-500

Values of individual cards

+20 points each -20 penalty

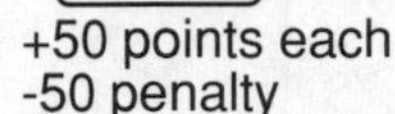

+50 points each
-50 penalty

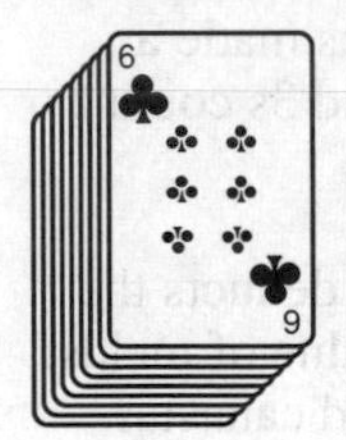

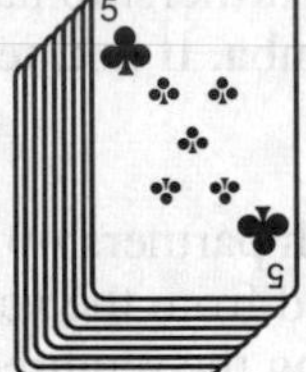

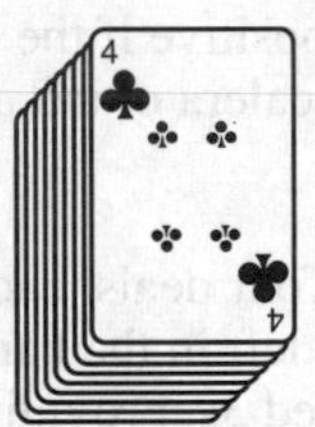

+5 points each
-5 penalty

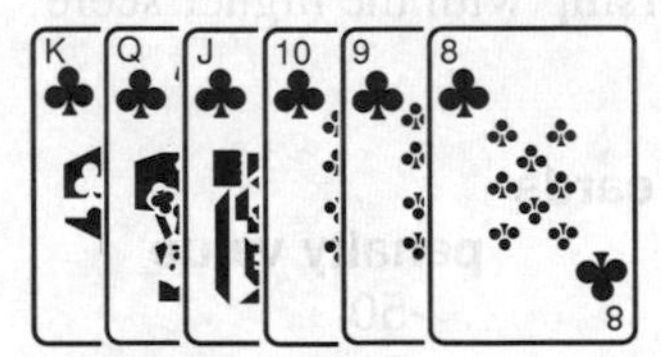

+10 points each
-10 penalty

+5 points each
-500 penalty

+2000 for all 6
-2000 penalty

+100 points each
-100 penalty
-500 if undeclared

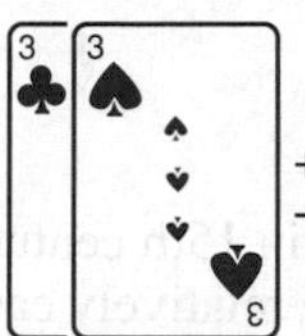

+5 points each
-200 penalty

Canastas in combo-canasta

Bolivia (wild)
2000 points

Escalera (sequence)
1500 points

Samba (7s)
1500 points

Mixed 7s
1000 points

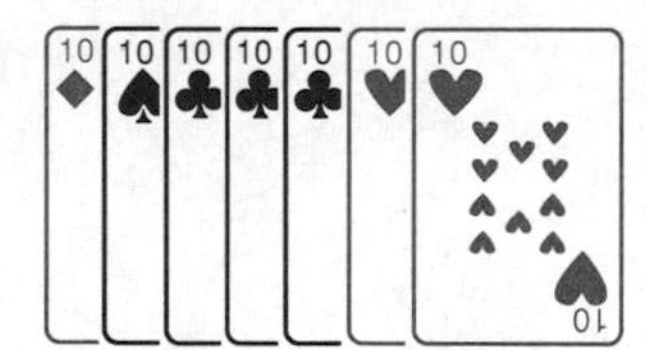

Red canasta (natural)
500 points

Black canasta (mixed)
300 points

Casino

Originating in 15th century France, this gambling game, while relatively easy to learn, requires skill with numbers.

Players

Two, three or four people can play.

Cards

The standard deck of 52 cards is used, the ace ranking low at a face value of 1. All other cards count at face value. Court cards have no numerical denomination.

Aim

Individuals score by capturing certain cards.

Dealing

The player making the lowest cut becomes the dealer.

Two players: the non-dealer gets two cards face down, two cards are placed face up on the table and two are dealt face down to the dealer. This is repeated until both players have a hand of four cards and four are face up on the table.
Three or four players: two cards are dealt face down to every player, including the dealer, then two face up on the table. This process is repeated once more.

Playing

The player to the dealer's left begins by playing at least one card to 'capture', 'build' or 'trail' cards. The others then play in turn by clockwise rotation.

Four ways of capturing cards

a A pair can be made by capturing a face-up card with the same numerical value as a card in the hand. The player puts his card face down on the captured card and pulls them towards him.
Two or more face-up cards can be captured if a player holds a card to match each of them in value.

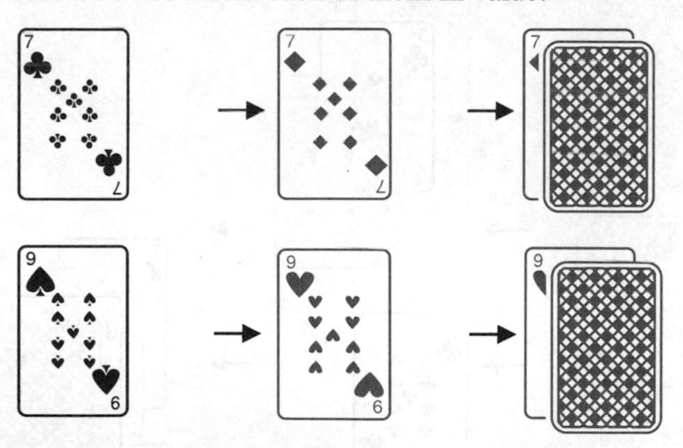

b A group can be made by capturing two or more cards totalling the numerical value of a card in the hand.

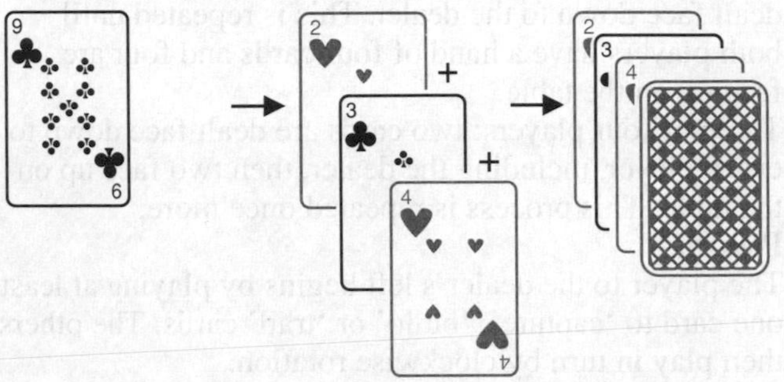

c A group and a pair can be made by capturing a group of two or three cards with the same value as one of the player's cards as well as a single card with the same value. A sweep is the capture of all four face-up cards in one turn.

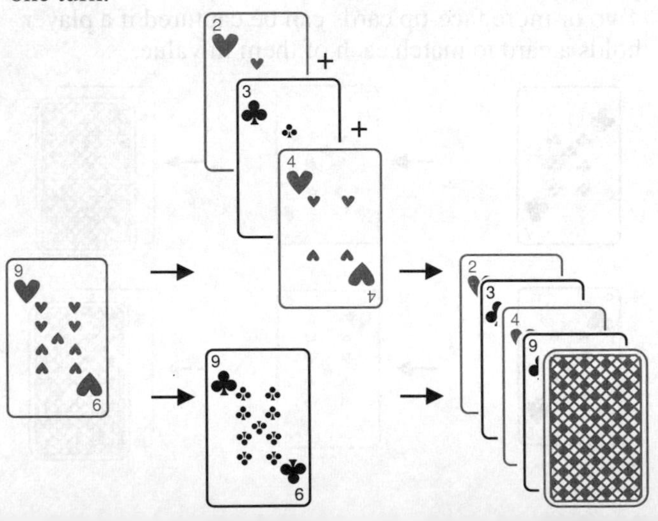

d Court cards can be captured by making a pair or a group of all four, providing a matching court card is held. A group cannot be made with only three court cards.

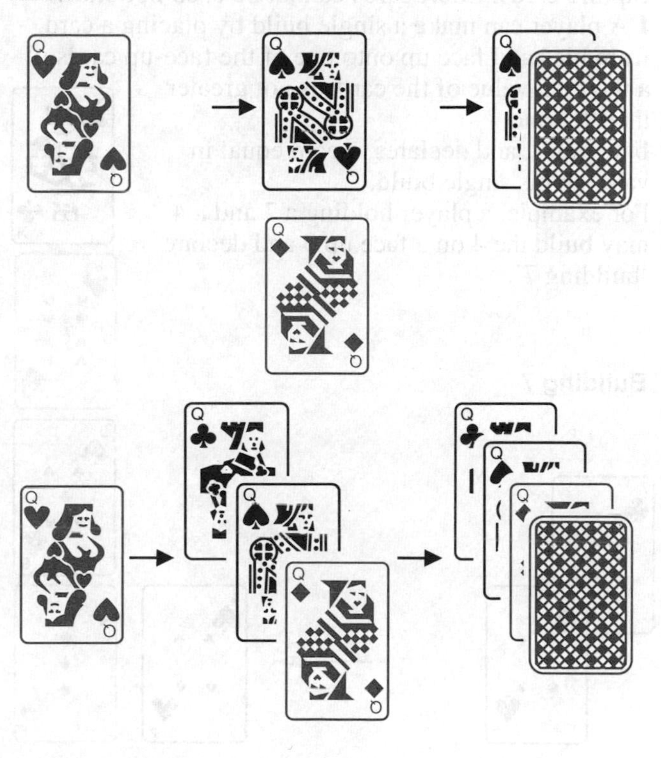

Two ways of building

Face-up cards can be built on by adding cards from the hand. The purpose of building is to make it possible to capture cards. Court cards cannot be used in builds.

1 A player can make a single build by placing a card from his hand face up onto one of the face-up cards if:

a the total value of the cards is not greater than 10; and

b he holds, and declares, a card equal in value to his single build.

For example, a player holding a 7 and a 4 may build the 4 on a face up 3 and declare 'building 7'.

Building 7

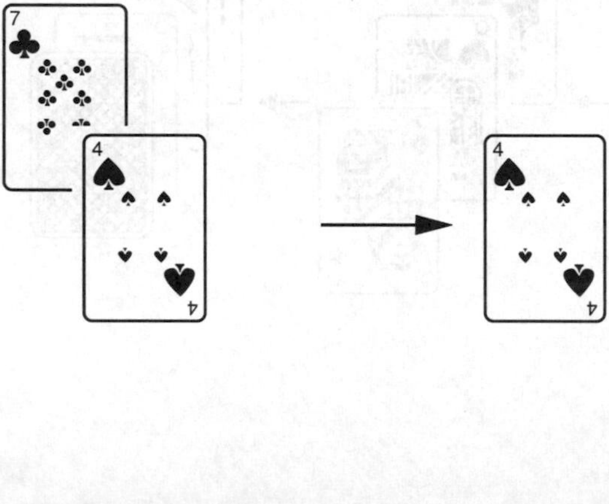

Subsequently another player holding an ace and an 8 may, in turn, build the ace onto the 3+4 and declare ‘building 8’. Cards being built remain in the centre of the table.

Building 8

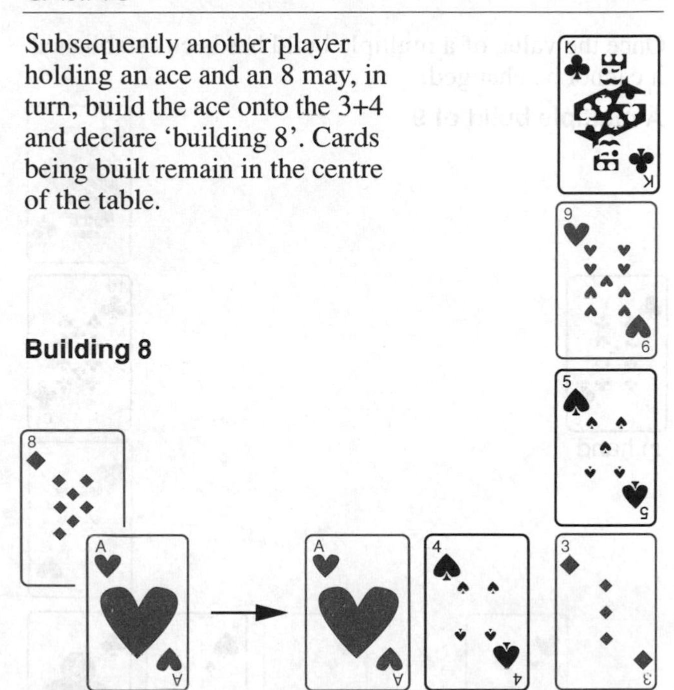

2 A player may also change an existing single build into a multiple build. This is done by increasing the value of an existing single build and then using other cards to add another build of the same value, placing it at the side of the first build.
For example, a multiple build of 9 could be made on an existing single build of 5 by a player who holds a 4, plus 4, 5 and 9. He would declare ‘building 9s’. His aim is to use his 9 to capture all the cards in his next turn, hoping that nobody else captures it first.

Once the value of a multiple build has been established it cannot be changed.

A multiple build of 9

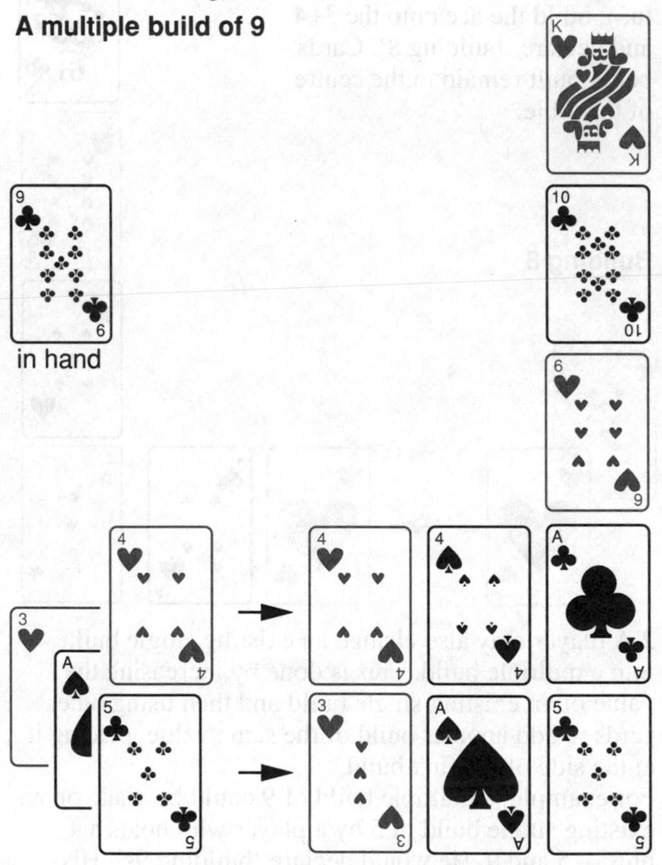

When a player has made or added to a build, in his next turn he must:
a capture the build; or
b add to a build; or
c make a new build.
He is only exempt from these obligations if an opponent captures or builds before him.

Trailing

A player who cannot capture or build then trails by adding one card from his hand to the face-up cards on the table.

Renewing the hand

When all players have no cards left they are dealt another four cards each in packets of two, but no more are dealt to the centre of the table. New face-up cards can only come from a player who trails.

Completing a round

When the pack runs out, any cards remaining face up are claimed by the player who made the last capture.
For each new round, players take the deal in turn.
Six rounds complete a game.

Scoring

Only captured cards score points, as follows:

2 of spades (little casino):	1
10 of diamonds (big casino):	2
Each ace:	1
Seven or more spades:	1
27 or more cards:	3
A sweep:	1

Winning the game

The winner is the player who gets the highest score in one round, or 21 points over several rounds.

ROYAL CASINO

Court cards are given numerical values and can be captured and used to build. The court cards count:

Js:	11
Qs:	12
Ks:	13

Aces may remain as 1 or may count as 14.

DRAW CASINO

Only the first 12 cards are dealt (for two players); after that players draw from the stock to replenish cards in their hands.

SPADE CASINO

Identical to the basic game but with additional scoring for certain spades:

ace of spades:	2
J of spades:	2
2 of spades:	2
Other spades:	1

The game is won by the player first gaining 61 points.

Cribbage

Thought to have been developed by Sir John Suckling, a poet and member of the English court in the early 17th century, cribbage requires a quick mind.

Players

The most popular game is six-card cribbage for two players. There are variations for three or four players as well.

Cards

A standard 52-card deck is used, all cards having their face value (ace is 1) and court cards counting 10.

The cribbage board

Although pencil and paper can be used for scoring, a cribbage board is much simpler. Usually a block of wood 25 cm by 8cm (10in by 3in), the board has four rows of 30 holes, in six groups of five pairs, two rows per player. At each end of the board are one or two game holes where the players keep their scoring pegs.

Moving the pegs to score

Each player uses two pegs, moving them alternately, first along the outer row and then along the inner.

a The first score is marked by moving a peg the same number of holes along the outer row of holes.

b The second score is marked by using a second peg to mark out the same number of holes beyond the first peg.

c The third score is marked by using the first peg to count that score beyond the second peg.

d To mark the next score, the peg that is behind is used to mark the score onwards from the front peg. Scoring continues until the front peg reaches the game hole by passing the end of the inner row.

Cribbage board

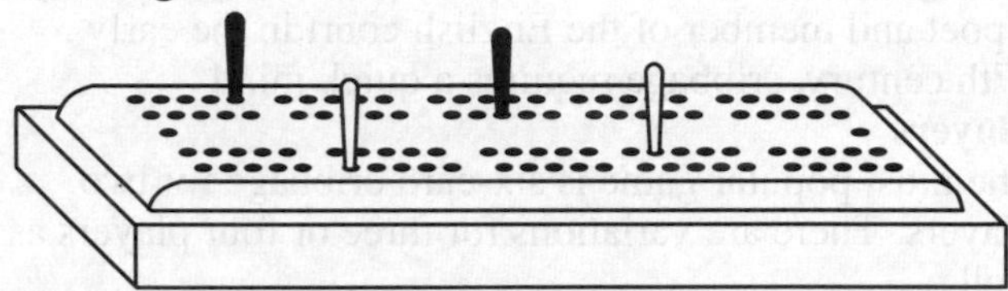

Scoring with pegs

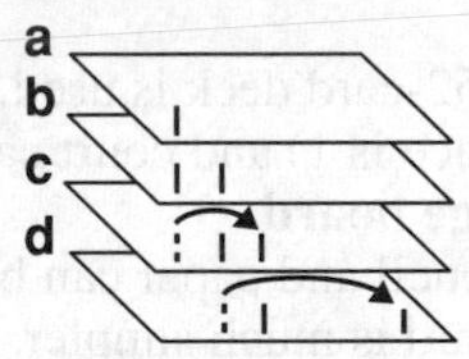

SIX-CARD CRIBBAGE (for two players)

Aim

The first player to go twice round the board, getting 121 points, wins the game.

Dealing

Players cut the deck and the one with the lower cut is first dealer. He deals six cards, face down and one at a time, to each player, beginning with his opponent. The rest of the deck is put aside.

The crib

Each player then discards two cards and places them face down to the right of the dealer to form the crib. The dealer will claim it as part of his score.

The cut

After the crib has been made, the non-dealer cuts the remaining deck. The top card is turned over by the dealer and left face up on the pack to be the start or starter. If this card is a J, two points 'for his heels' are scored by the dealer.

Scoring

Points can be scored for groups of cards made during play and when the hand is shown at the end. The following groups of cards score points:

a Pair (two cards of the same rank):	2
b Pair royal (three of the same rank):	6
c Double pair royal (all four cards of the same rank):	12
d Run (a sequence of cards in rank order):	1 point per card of any suit
e Flush (any four or five cards of the same suit):	1 point per card

If also a run, it scores for both flush and run.

f Fifteen (any group of cards with a total face value of 15):	2

Scoring

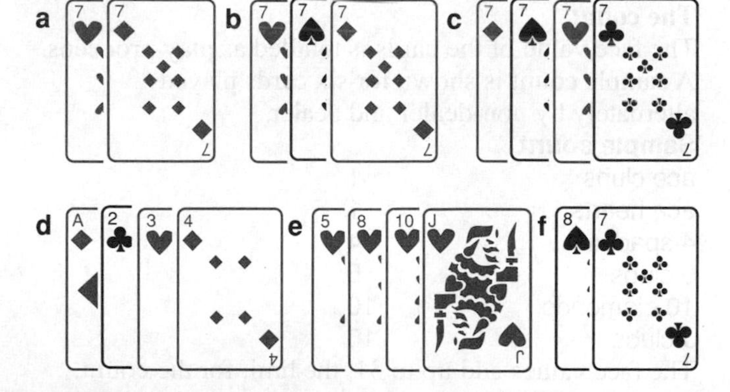

Playing

The non-dealer places one card from his hand face up in front of him and calls out its numerical value. The dealer then does the same.

The players continue to call as they add a card to their own spread of cards in turn, scoring for a pair, pair royal, run or fifteen they make with their opponent's card during play. Flushes are not taken into account during play.

Examples of some calls

player	card	call	score
non-dealer	ace	'one'	0
dealer	2	'run for two' (ace, 1)	2
non-dealer	4	'four'	0
dealer	5	'run for two'	2
non-dealer	3	'fifteen for seven'	7

The non-dealer makes seven points from a fifteen: 1+2+4+5+3=15 (two points) plus a run: ace, 2, 4, 5, 3 (five points). Cards in a run do not have to have been played in the correct order.

The count

The face value of the cards is totalled as play proceeds. A sample count is shown for six cards played alternately by non-dealer and dealer.

Sample count

ace clubs	1
ace hearts	1
4 spades	4
5 clubs	5
10 diamonds	10
J clubs	10

The face values add up to 31, the limit for the count.

The player whose card reaches a count of 31 scores two extra points and both players' face-up cards are turned face down.

A player who cannot keep the count within 31 at his turn must call 'go'.

The opponent then plays any card low enough to keep the total below 31. If the count then reaches 31, he gets two points; if it is still less than 31, he gets one point and calls 'go'.

Play begins again, but with only the cards remaining in the hands, and continues until the count reaches 31 or all cards have been played. The player of the last card of a hand gains 'one for the last'.

The show

When all four cards of the hand have been played, the non-dealer begins the show by picking up his cards and showing the scores he can make with them.

If the non-dealer is close to reaching the winning score of 121, being the first to show can be an advantage.

He then organizes his cards in any combination for scoring (see Scoring **a** to **f**.) Both players can include the start card in their show. For example, if the start card is 4 hearts and a player has 4 clubs, 5 hearts, 6 clubs and 6 spades, the scoring combinations of 4, 4, 5, 6, 6 are:

8 points for fifteen (four combinations of 4, 5, 6);
12 points for runs (four runs of 4, 5, 6); and
4 points for pairs (5, 5, and 6, 6);
making a total of 24 points.

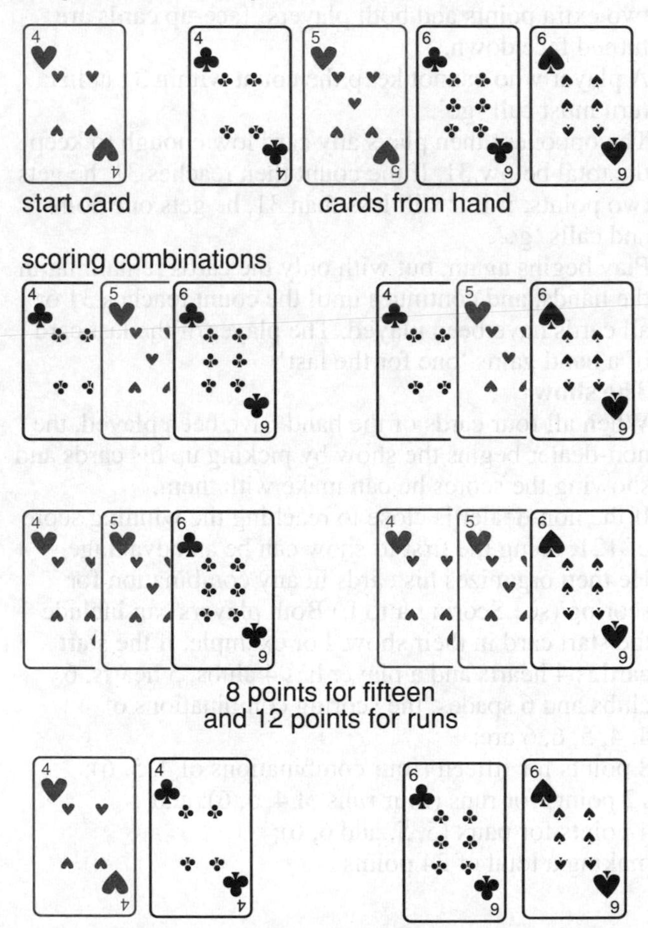
Sample show of 24 points
start card
cards from hand
scoring combinations
8 points for fifteen
and 12 points for runs
4 points for pairs

Scoring cards of the same suit

A player holding a J of the same suit as the start card scores 'one for his nob'.

A player holding a flush of four cards of the same suit scores four points, but a four-card flush cannot be made with the start card. However, the start card can be added to make a flush of five, scoring five points.

When the non-dealer has finished scoring his cards, the dealer does the same with first his own cards and then with the cards in the crib. The crib is scored like a hand, but only a five-card flush is counted. The dealer adds the crib score to his own.

Five-card flush in hearts

start card cards in hand

Conventions

A redeal is required if there are errors in dealing. If a dealing mistake is found after play has begun, the non-dealer gains two points and the cards are redealt or extra cards are drawn from the stock pile.

If a player does not play his extra cards after a call of 'go', he may not play those cards later and his opponent gains two points. There are no penalties for counting errors during play.

A player scores an extra game in his favour if he reaches a score of 121 before his opponent is halfway

round the board – i.e., before he reaches 61. This is called a 'lurch'.
In a rule not always used, a player may call his opponent 'muggins' when he has missed a score he could have made. The player can then add the missed score to his own.

FIVE-CARD CRIBBAGE

The rules are as for six-card cribbage with the following exceptions:

1 the aim is to win a game of 61 points;
2 five cards are dealt to each player; and
3 to compensate for not having the crib, the non-dealer pegs three points at the beginning.

SEVEN-CARD CRIBBAGE

Seven cards are dealt to each player and 181 points wins the game. Otherwise the rules are as for six-card cribbage.

THREE-HANDED CRIBBAGE

Five cards are dealt to each player, only one of which goes to the crib. The game is 61 points and there is no 31-point limit. The player to the left of the dealer both leads play and has the first show. Otherwise the rules are as for basic six-card cribbage.

FOUR-HANDED CRIBBAGE

This is the basic six-card game for partners, who sit opposite each other and play against the other partnership. The deal is usually five cards to each player, of which only one goes to the crib.

Hearts

A 19th-century game in which players try to avoid taking penalty cards.

Players

Any number from three to seven people, each playing for themselves.

Cards

The standard 52-card deck is used. Ace ranks high and there are no trump cards. The 2s are stripped from the deck according to the number of players. The 2 of hearts is always retained.

One card played by each person in turn makes a trick.

Table of numbers

players	stripped cards	cards in a trick
three	one 2	3
four	none	4
five	two 2s	5
six	three 2s	6
seven	three 2s	7

Rank

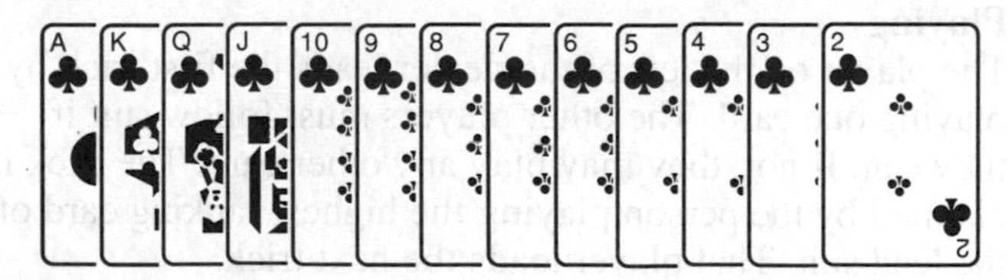

Aim

Players make tricks and score penalty points for every hearts card they use. Thus the aim is to score zero by avoiding the use of heart cards in tricks.

Preparing

Paper and pencil will be needed for scoring penalty points. Players should agree beforehand how the game is to be won. The options are:

1 the game ends when one person reaches a penalty score of 50 points; or

2 the game ends when an agreed number of rounds have been played, usually four or five.

Dealing

The player making the lowest cut becomes the dealer. Beginning with the player on his left, he deals the cards face down, singly, to each player in clockwise rotation, until all the cards are dealt.

Number of cards in each hand

players	deck	hand
three	51	17
four	52	13
five	50	10
six	49	8 (The last card is put aside.)
seven	49	7

Playing

The player on the left of the dealer leads the first trick by playing one card. The other players must follow suit if they can. If not, they may play any other card. The trick is claimed by the person playing the highest ranking card of the lead suit. That player leads the next trick.

The hand ends when all 13 heart cards have been played, unless a player fails to correct a revoke.

Revoking

If a player revokes – i.e., fails to follow suit when he could have – he may correct his mistake before the trick is claimed. Otherwise he scores 13 penalty points and the round ends immediately. No penalties are scored by the other players.
The deal for the next round passes clockwise to the player on the left of the last dealer.

Scoring

At the end of each round, every heart card in a player's tricks counts as one penalty point. Any cards left in the hand do not count.

Cards scoring one penalty point

Winning the game

The winner is the player with the lowest number of penalty points at the agreed stage of the game – i.e., after a player has scored 50 points or the agreed number of rounds has been played (see Preparing).

HEARTS VARIATIONS

These eight popular variations of hearts are all played the same as the basic game with differences as indicated.

SPOT HEARTS

A scoring variation, each heart card counts as its face value.

Spot hearts penalty points

card	penalty score
ace	1
K	13
Q	12
J	11
10 to 2	face value

Penalty cards

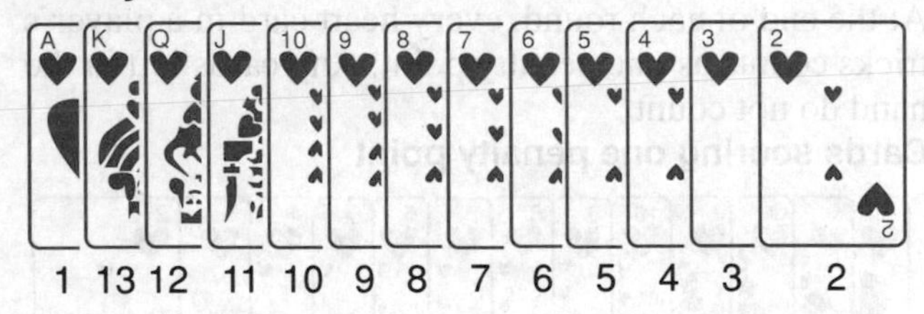

BLACK LADY

13 penalty points

The Q of spades is an extra penalty card valued at 13 points. A player with the Q of spades in his hand must use it as soon as possible. All hearts score one penalty point as in the basic game.

GREEK HEARTS

After the first deal of a game, each player examines his hand and chooses three cards to pass, face down, to the player on his right. A player may only look at the cards he is receiving after he has passed his own cards. The Q of spades is used as an extra penalty card and penalty points are scored as shown.

Greek hearts penalty points

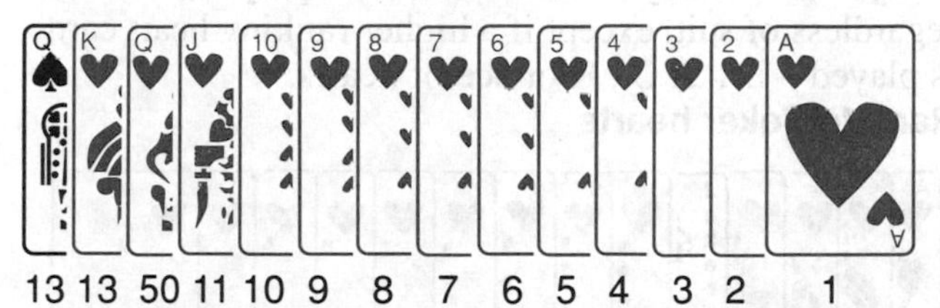

A player who takes tricks containing all 14 penalty cards makes a zero score. When this happens, all other players score 150 penalty points regardless of which cards they have played.

DOMINO HEARTS

Each player is dealt only six cards and the rest form a stock pile, face down.

Players draw a card from the stock when they cannot follow suit, and continue drawing until they can, keeping all the extra cards to use in play. When the stock is finished, players then discard, as in basic hearts.

As players use up their cards, they drop out. The last player left in then counts one penalty point for each heart card in both his tricks and his hand. The others all score one penalty point for heart cards in their tricks.

The game ends when one player reaches a penalty score of 31. The winner is the player with the lowest score.

JOKER HEARTS

The 2 of hearts is removed from the deck and the joker is included, ranking below the J of hearts. All heart cards carry one penalty point each, as in the basic game of hearts. However, the joker scores five penalty points.

The joker wins any trick in which it is played, regardless of suit, except if a higher ranking heart card is played – i.e., J, Q , K or ace of hearts.

Rank for joker hearts

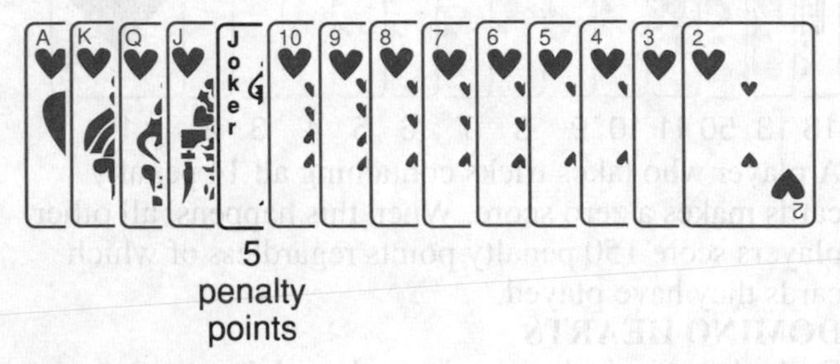

HEARTSETTE

A widow hand is placed face down on the table and remains there. The number of cards depends on the number of players, as shown in the table.

Cards in the widow

players	widow	deck
three	3	51 (2 of spades removed)
four	3	51 (2 of spades removed)
five	2	52
six	4	52
seven	3	52

After the widow has been dealt, all other cards are dealt among the players. The first person to make a trick also takes the widow and scores penalty points for any hearts in it.

HEARTS FOR TWO

Each player is dealt 13 cards; the rest form a stock. The winner of each trick takes the top card from the stock and the loser takes the next card.

The game ends when all cards have been played. Scoring is as for basic hearts.

BLACK MARIA

The game (also called Slippery Anne) is the same as basic hearts, but there are three extra cards carrying high penalty points:

Black Maria, the Q of spades:	13 points
the K of spades:	10 points
the ace of spades:	7 points

An exchange of three cards from each player to the person on his right takes place before play, as in Greek hearts.

When all penalty cards have been played, the round ends.

Penalty cards in Black Maria

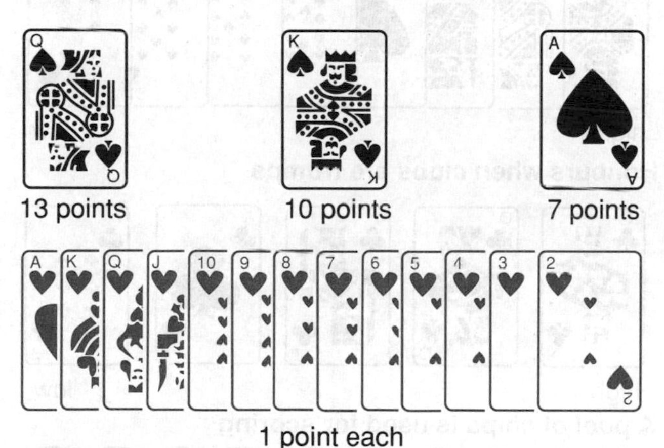

Imperial

A game for two players, similar to piquet.

Cards

Imperial requires a piquet deck of 32 cards, made by stripping 6s, 5s, 4s, 3s and 2s from a 52-card deck. The cards rank from high to low: K, Q, J, ace, 10, 9, 8, 7. The trump suit is declared for each hand. The K, Q, J, ace and 7 of trumps are the honour cards.
Cards count their face value; aces count 11 and court cards count 10 each.

Rank

high low

Honours when clubs are trumps

high low

A pool of chips is used for scoring

Chips
For each point scored, one white chip is taken. When a player has six white chips, he trades them for one red. When a player gains a red chip, his opponent loses all his white chips back to the pool.

Aim
Players try to win five red chips from the pool by scoring before, during and after play in each deal.

Dealing
Players cut for deal. The dealer shuffles and the non-dealer cuts. Cards are dealt face down in four packets of three, beginning with the non-dealer.
When both players have 12 cards, the next (25th) card determines trumps for that deal and is placed face up. The remaining cards are set aside.

Scoring before play
1 If the turned-up trump card is an honour card, the dealer scores one white chip.
2 If a hand is carte blanche (contains no K, Q or J), the player scores one red chip.
3 Combinations of cards are then declared and scored.
4 Combinations including the upcard are declared and scored last of all.

Scores for combinations
Cards can be combined as 'points', sequences or melds and are declared and scored in that order. A player can use any card in his hand in more than one combination.
A point is the suit in which a player holds the greatest number of cards. The player with the longer suit scores the point and claims one white chip for each card.
In case of a draw, the player whose point has the higher

total face value scores. If there is still a draw, the non-dealer gains the score.

Sample scoring for points

dealer's point non-dealer's point

point score:
5 white chips 5 white chips

result: a draw

value score:
7+8+10+11+10 = 46 7+10+10+10 +10 = 47

non-dealer wins points score of 5 white chips

A sequence is a run of three or four consecutive cards (the K, Q, J or ace only) of the same suit. Four cards beat three and the higher ranking card sequence wins one red chip. The non-dealer scores in a draw.

Sample sequences

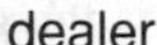
dealer non-dealer

K ranks higher than a Q so dealer wins one red chip for the best sequence

Melds are groups of cards of the same rank. In imperial, a combination of four Ks, four Qs, four Js, four aces or four 7s form a meld and rank in that order with K high. The best meld scores one red chip.

Sample melds

dealer

non-dealer

Q ranks higher than J so non-dealer wins one red chip for the best meld.

How to declare combinations

Combinations are declared formally, to avoid giving the opponent too much information.

The non-dealer begins in each of the three declarations: points, sequence and meld.

Point declaration

1 Non-dealer: 'A point of...' (states number).

2 Dealer has three possible replies:

a 'Good' if he concedes.

b 'Not good' if his point is longer. He then states the length of his point and the score he claims.

c 'How many?' if his point is the same length.

3 If the dealer asked 'how many?' the non-dealer then states the face value of his point.

4 Dealer answers 'good' if he concedes; 'not good' if the face value of his point is larger; or 'equal' if the value of his point is the same. In this case, the non-dealer scores.

5 The winner then declares the length and face value of his point and claims the score.

Sample points declaration

dealer's point non-dealer's point

value: 46 value: 47

Non-dealer: 'A point of five.'
Dealer: 'How many?'
Non-dealer: 'Value 47.'
Dealer: 'Good.'
Non-dealer: 'A point of five, value 47, I score five.'

Sequence declaration

The non-dealer begins by declaring: 'A sequence of....' He states the number and the procedure continues as in points declaration.

Sample sequence declaration

Non-dealer: 'A sequence of three.'
Dealer: 'How high?'
Non-dealer: 'Queen.'
Dealer: 'Not good. King. I score one.'

Meld declaration
The non-dealer begins by declaring: 'Four...,' stating the suit of his meld. The procedure continues as before, with the dealer replying:
'Good' if he concedes;
'Not good' if he holds a meld of a higher ranking card or his meld trumps his opponent's; or
'Equal' if he has a meld of the same denomination.

Sample meld declaration

non-dealer dealer

Non-dealer: 'Four aces.'
Dealer: 'Good.'
Non-dealer: 'Four aces. I score one.'

Adding point, sequence and meld scores
Each player adds the score for the previous declaration to the current one. Taking the samples given above, the accumulated scores would be declared as follows:
Non-dealer: 'A point of five.'
Dealer: 'How many?'
Non-dealer: 'Value 47.'
Dealer: 'Good.'
Non-dealer: 'A point of five, value 47, I score five. (pause) A sequence of three.'
Dealer: 'How high?'
Non-dealer: 'Queen.'
Dealer: 'Not good. King. I score one.'

Non-dealer: 'Four aces.'
Dealer: 'Good.'
Non-dealer: 'Four aces. I score five.' He then totals his score and says, 'I start with...,' stating his total, which will be 10 plus another 5 if he was dealt a carte blanche.
The dealer ends up with no score because he must return his white chip to the pool when the non-dealer wins his second red chip.
Finally, sequence and melds using the upcard are declared and scored in the same manner.

Playing

The first trick is led by the non-dealer; each trick is then led by the winner of the previous one.
The second player must take the trick if possible and must follow suit if he can. If he can't, he must trump it. If he can do neither, he is allowed to discard.
Tricks remain face up on the table in front of the player who won them; he is free to examine them.

Scoring during play

One red chip is won:
1 by a player using a K or Q to take the J of trumps;
2 by a player taking the ace.
One white chip is won for every trump honour card included in the tricks a player wins.

Scoring at the end of play

The player with the most tricks wins one white chip for each trick in excess of his opponent's.
Two red chips are gained by a player winning all 12 tricks, called the capot.

Winning the game

The game is won by the player who first gets five red chips. If this happens during play, the hand is abandoned.

Klaberjass

Very similar to the French championship game of belotte, klaberjass – also known as kalabriasz, Kolobiosh, klab or clobber – is an interesting game for two players.

Cards

A 52-card deck is stripped of all 6s, 5s, 4s, 3s and 2s to produce a 32-card deck. The ranking is unusual both in plain and trump suits as shown. The 7 of trumps is called the dix.

Ranking in all plain suits

Ranking when a suit is trumps

Aim

Each player tries to reach a score of 500 points by melding sequences and taking tricks containing high scoring cards.

Dealing

The first dealer is chosen by high cut using standard ranking with ace low. After the shuffle and cut, six cards are dealt face down to each player in two packets of three. The next card is turned up in the centre of the table and the remaining cards placed next to it, face down, as the stock.

Bidding for trumps

There are three ways of bidding:

1 'Accept' means the suit of the central upcard is trumps.

2 'Pass' means the bidding passes to the next player.

3 'Schmeiss' means a new deal is proposed.

The non-dealer begins the bidding. If his bid is pass, it becomes the dealer's turn to bid.

If his bid is schmeiss, the dealer then has to choose between agreeing to a new deal or making a bid of accept. He may also pass, leading to a new round of bids.

If the dealer chooses to bid accept, the non-dealer then has to accept or pass. If he passes, the dealer then has a second bid.

If the dealer also passes in this second round, the bidding ends and there is a new deal.

The maker is the name given to the player who wins the bid by determining trumps.

The second deal

When trumps have been determined, three more cards are dealt to each player singly.

The bottom card is then taken from the stock and placed face up on top of the pile. A player who holds the dix (7 of trumps) may exchange it for this top card, providing trumps were determined by the acceptance of the central upcard.

Players then examine their cards to find which sequences they are holding.

Sequences

A sequence is a consecutive run of three or more cards of the same suit.

A three-card sequence scores 20 points.

A sequence of four or more scores 50 points.

The rank order for sequence building is ace, K, Q, J, 10, 9, 8, 7. When sequences are of the same value, they rank according to their highest value card. All trump cards outrank plain suit cards.

If two sequences in plain suits are still of equal value, neither player scores. Some people vary this rule and make the non-dealer's sequence the highest.

Sequences

20 points

50 points

Declaring sequences

This is usually done before play starts, but may be done after the non-dealer has started play by placing his lead card to the first trick. The declaration is to show which player holds the higher sequence.

The non-dealer starts by declaring:

a 'sequence of 20' for a three-card sequence; or

b 'sequence of 50' for one of four or more.

The dealer replies:
a 'good' if he concedes;
b 'not good' if he can declare a higher sequence; or
c 'how high?' if he has a sequence of the same value.
In this case the non-dealer declares the highest ranking card of his sequence.
In reply the dealer declares 'good' or 'not good.'

Scoring the winning sequence

The player who has declared the highest sequence must then show it before claiming the score. He may also score for any other sequences he holds, providing he shows them. The other player gets no score at this stage.

Playing

The first trick is led by the non-dealer and the suit must be followed, trumped or a discard played, in that order. If the leading suit is trumps, it must be trumped if possible. The player winning the trick claims it and leads to the next trick.

Bella

A player who holds the K and Q of trumps is said to hold the bella. It is worth 20 points, but only when each card has been played to take a trick. If the player also holds the J of trumps, he scores for both the bella and the sequence.

The bella when clubs are trumps

Scoring during play

When a player takes one of the following cards in tricks, he scores accordingly:

the jasz (J of trumps):	20 points
the menel (9 of trumps):	14 points
aces:	11 points
10s:	10 points
Ks:	4 points
Qs:	3 points
Js (except the jasz):	2 points

The last trick scores 10 points for the player taking it.

Scoring during play when spades are trumps

trumps; jazs 20 points; menel 14 points; 11 points; 10 points; 4 points; 3 points; plain suits 2 points

Scoring the hand

After all nine tricks have been taken, the score for the hand is made as follows:

1 If the maker (the player who won the trumps bid)

has the higher score, both players keep their own scores.
2 If the maker's opponent has the higher score, he 'goes bate' by scoring both his own and the maker's total.
3 If both players have the same points total, the maker 'goes half bate' by scoring nil, and his opponent keeps his own score.

Winning the game

The first player to reach 500 points wins the game.
If both players reach 500 points in the same hand, the one with the higher final score wins.

THREE-HANDED KLABERJASS

The deal and play rotate clockwise around the table.
The maker must go bate or score more than the sum of his opponents' scores.
Sequences and points scored in play are kept individually, but if the maker goes bate, the opponents share his points.

FOUR-HANDED KLABERJASS

The deal and play proceed clockwise. Everyone is dealt eight cards, except the dealer who gets seven.
The player holding the dix trades it for the central up card, as in the standard game, but the dealer then takes the dix as the eighth card in his hand.
The partner of the player who has declared the highest sequence also scores his own sequences.
Partners combine their scores and keep their tricks together. The rules for winning the game are as for the standard game, the two partnerships scoring as if they were two players.

Michigan

A fast-moving, challenging game for beginners and experienced players alike. Michigan is played for stakes by three to eight people. It is also known as Boodle, Chicago, Newmarket or Saratoga.

Cards

A standard 52-card deck is used, with ace ranking high. The J of spades, Q of diamonds, K of clubs and ace of hearts from another pack form the 'boodle'. These four cards are placed separately, face up, in the centre of the table.

Boodle cards

Preparing

Players cut the cards for sitting positions, the one drawing the highest card having first choice and the others sitting clockwise in order of cut. Everyone begins with the same number of counters or chips. Players should decide how the game is to be won by agreeing:

a a time limit for the game;
b how many deals shall be played; or
c how many chips shall be the winning number.

Aim

Each player tries to gain chips by playing cards matching the boodle and by being the first to play all his cards.

Ante

Players ante by placing one chip on each boodle card before the deal for each hand.

Dealing

The player making the highest cut becomes the first dealer. Subsequent deals rotate clockwise.

The whole pack is dealt, singly and face down, starting with an extra hand to the dealer's left, known as the widow. All hands should have an equal number of cards, though the pack may not divide evenly due to the number of players.

The auction

Before play, the dealer can exchange his hand for the widow and discard his own hand face down.

If the dealer does not take the widow, the others may bid for it. The player making the highest bid pays chips to the dealer, takes the widow and discards his own hand face down.

If nobody bids for the widow, it remains face down.

Playing

The player to the dealer's left lays down his lowest card face up in front of him, announcing its rank and suit. Whoever holds the next higher card in the same suit plays it in the same way in front of himself. This may be the same player.

Cards continue to be played in sequence, by whichever player holds them, until the ace is played or nobody has the next card.

Each player has his own pile of face-up cards, but once he has covered a card, it cannot be examined again.

Stopping play

When a sequence ends, play is 'stopped' and the last player begins a new sequence with the lowest card he has in another suit. If he cannot do so, play passes to the next person sitting clockwise. If nobody can play, the original player may start a new sequence in the same suit as before.

Boodle winnings

If someone plays a card the same as a boodle card, he takes all the chips on that card. If nobody claims any of the boodle chips, they remain in place.

Before every new deal, each player antes a chip onto each boodle card.

End of play

When one player has used all his cards, play ends. The other players must then pay him one chip for every card they hold.

Penalty

When a card that should be is not played in sequence, that player pays one chip to each opponent. If his failure has prevented someone else from gaining boodle chips, he must use his own chips to make good the loss. The boodle chips remaining are carried over to the next hand.

Winning the game

As decided during preparation for play, the winner is either:

a the first person to gain an agreed number of chips; or

b the player holding the most chips after an agreed time or an agreed number of deals.

Napoleon

Similar to euchre, napoleon (or nap) is a game for two to seven people who each play alone for stakes, using counters.

Aim

The highest bidder attempts to fulfil his contract by taking tricks while the other players try to prevent him.

Cards

A standard deck of 52 cards is used, with ace ranking high.

Dealing

The player making the highest cut becomes the first dealer. Subsequent deals rotate clockwise.

Five cards are dealt, face down and singly, to each player. The remainder is placed face down to form the stock.

Rank

Bidding

The player to the left of the dealer begins the bidding. He can pass or bid to make two, three, four or five tricks. Five tricks is called a napoleon. Players bid in turn and must make a higher bid than the previous one. There is only one round of bidding, and the 'bidder' is the person who makes the highest bid.

Playing

The bidder begins play with one card, the suit of which becomes trumps for that hand.

Each person in turn plays one card, following suit if possible. If not, any other card may be played. The trick contains one card from each player and is won by the person who plays:

a the highest trump card; or

b the highest card of the leading suit.

Play continues until all five tricks have been made.

Scoring

The usual stakes are:

a two counters for a bid of two

b three counters for a bid of three

c four counters for a bid of four

d ten counters for a bid of napoleon

The other players each pay the bidder these stakes if he fulfils his contract. If he does not, he must pay each player the stake instead, except if he bid napoleon, in which case he pays each player half the stake.

Optional bids

Sometimes the game is played with the following bids:

a 'Wellington' is a bid to win all five tricks for double stakes (20 counters). A wellington can only be bid following a bid of napoleon.

b 'Blücher' will outbid a wellington for triple the stakes (30 counters).

c 'Misère' or 'misery' is a bid to lose every trick and ranks between a bid of three and a bid of four. It carries a stake of three counters. Misery is played without trumps.

PURCHASE NAP

The rules are as for napoleon, except that on payment of one counter per card, any player may exchange one or more of his cards for unseen cards from the top of the stock. The payments are set aside in a kitty to be won by the first player to fulfil a bid of napoleon.

SEVEN-CARD NAP

Play is the same as for napoleon, but each player is dealt seven cards and there are no bids of wellington or blücher.

The rank order of bids and their stakes is:

a three bid: stake three
b four bid: stake four
c nap or misère bid: stake ten
d six bid: stake 18
e seven bid: stake 24

Only half the stake is paid if a player loses a bid of nap, misère, six or seven.

Oh Hell

Similar to whist, oh hell is a game for three or more players, each playing alone. Oh hell is also known as blackout, and by some as oh well.

Cards

A standard 52-card deck is used, with ace ranking high.

Rank

Aim

Every player makes a bid for tricks, which he tries to fulfil exactly.

Dealing

The player making the highest cut becomes the first dealer. Subsequent deals pass clockwise; there are several deals in each game. In the first deal players are dealt one card each. In the next deal, players are dealt two cards each; in the third, three cards; and so on. When it is no longer possible to deal an extra card to each player, the game ends. For example, when there are four players there will be 13 deals; when there are five players, 10 deals.

Trumps

The top card from the stock is turned up at the end of each deal to designate trumps. When the last deal of the game allows for no stock, there are no trumps in that hand.

Bidding

The dealer begins by bidding the number of tricks he expects to win or bidding 'nullo' if he does not expect to make any.

In the first hand, the bid is one or nullo. The number of possible bids increases as the number of dealt cards increases.

Playing

The player to the dealer's left leads with any card. In the first hand he has no choice but to play the single card he has been dealt. The others must follow suit if they can. If not, they may trump or discard.

The player winning the trick claims it face down and leads to the next trick.

Scoring

Players who have fulfilled their bids exactly gain one point per trick plus a bonus of 10 points.

For fulfilling a bid of nullo, the score may be five points, or one point per trick in the hand plus five points. Players should agree beforehand which scoring system is to be used.

Players who make fewer or more than the number of tricks bid do not score or lose penalty points.

Optional scoring

A bonus of 25 points can be won by a player who fulfils a small slam bid by winning all but one of the hand's tricks, providing there are more than five cards in the hand.

A bonus of 50 points can be won by a player who makes a grand slam (all the tricks).

Winning the game

The player with the highest total score after all deals are played is the winner.

Piquet

This game offers two players the opportunity to use great skill. Known by various names since the 1450s, the game was given its French name and terminology by Charles I of England to honour Henrietta Maria, his French wife.

Modern piquet has some optional rules, sometimes called American style or English style. The options are described here when they occur. Most players generally choose one style and keep to it.

Cards

The piquet deck of 32 cards is used, which ranks normally with ace high. It is made by stripping the cards below 7 from a standard 52-card deck. Regular piquet players have two decks, one in use and the other ready shuffled for the next deal.

Rank

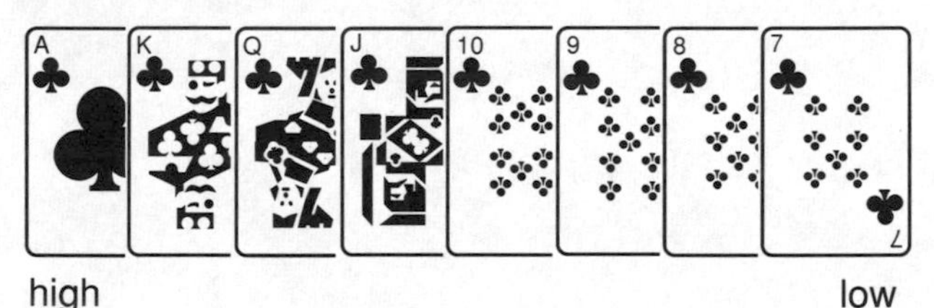

Aim

A player tries to score more points than his opponent by taking tricks and by collecting scoring combinations of cards.

Card values

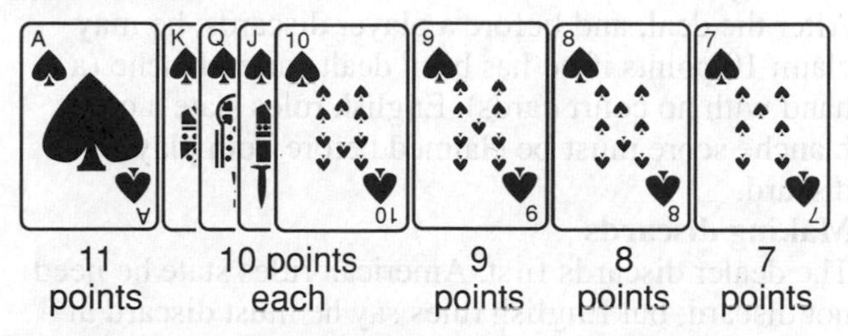

Dealing

The player cutting the higher card becomes first dealer and chooses his seat. The dealer shuffles the cards which are then cut by the non-dealer.

Beginning with the non-dealer, each player is dealt 12 cards in packets of two. A stock is formed from the remaining eight cards by turning the cards face down and dividing them so that the upper five lie at an angle to the lower three.

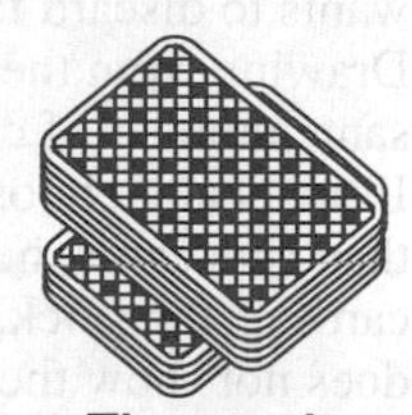

The stock

The partie

A game is known as a partie and normally consists of six deals. Each deal has four parts:

a making discards;
b deciding which scoring combinations to declare;
c announcing declarations; and
d playing for tricks.

Scoring takes place as the partie unfolds, so paper and pencil are essential for keeping the scores and cumulative totals.

Scoring before the discard

After the deal, and before a player discards, he may claim 10 points if he has been dealt carte blanche (a hand with no court cards). English rules state a carte blanche score must be claimed before both players discard.

Making discards

The dealer discards first. American rules state he need not discard, but English rules say he must discard at least one card. Either way, a player may only discard up to five cards.

If the dealer decides to discard, he places the cards he wants to discard face down near him.

Drawing from the top of the stock, in order, he takes the same number of cards into his hand.

If the dealer chooses not to discard, or discards fewer than five cards, he has the right to look at all five top cards of the stock, replacing them in the same order. He does not show the cards to his opponent.

The non-dealer must then discard one card and may discard more, up to the number remaining in the whole stock. He places them face down beside him and takes replacements into his hand from the top of the stock in order.

He can then inspect the cards (if any) that remain in the stock, but if he does, the dealer may also inspect them. (Some players only allow the dealer to inspect them later, after he has played his first trick.)

During play, both players may inspect their own discards at any time.

Combinations to declare

Players can make three kinds of combinations, using the cards in their hands. Any card may be included in more than one combination. The aim is to make high-scoring combinations which rank higher than the opponent's combinations.

A player may choose to 'sink' one or more of his combinations by not declaring it. No score can be claimed for any combination that has been sunk.

There are three types of combination, called 'point', 'sequence' and 'meld'.

A point is a collection of cards all of the same suit. The player with the biggest collection scores one point for each card in that suit.

If both players have a collection of the same number, the cards in each collection are counted at face value and the highest score wins the point value. If there is still a draw, neither player scores. A player can only score for one point, even if he holds two collections greater than his opponent's.

Ranking when point scores are the same

point score is 4
face value is 36
this point ranks higher

point score is 4
face value is 35
this point ranks lower

A sequence is a run of three or more cards in one suit in rank order. The player with the longest sequence scores for all the sequences he holds, as follows:

a three cards, a tierce: 3 points
b four cards, a quart: 4 points
c five cards, a quint: 15 points
d six cards, a sextet or sixième: 16 points
e seven cards, a septet or septième: 17 points
f eight cards , an octet or huitième: 18 points

The loser makes no score for any of his sequences.
If there is a draw, the sequence with the highest ranking top card wins. If there is still a draw, neither player scores.

Sample sequences in rank order

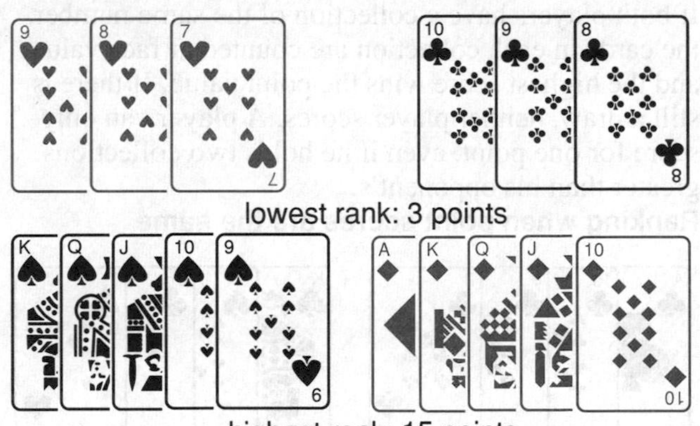

lowest rank: 3 points

highest rank: 15 points

A meld is three or four cards of the same kind in different suits. Only aces, Ks, Qs, Js and 10s may be used in melds. Some players only allow 10s in melds of four cards.

The player making the longest meld scores for all the melds he holds as follows:

a three cards, a trio: 3 points

b four cards, a quatorze or 'fourteen': 14 points

If both players have melds of the same length, the one with the highest ranking cards wins.

Sample melds

3 points

14 points

Announcing declarations

The announcements are made briefly and formally to avoid revealing too much information. Declarations are made in the order of points, sequences and then melds. (Some players prefer the French names for sequences and melds.) The non-dealer begins each dialogue.

Dialogue declaring a point

Non-dealer: 'A point of..., ' saying how many cards are in his longest suit.

Dealer replies with either:

a 'good' if he concedes the point;

b 'not good...,' stating how many cards in his point if it is longer; or

c 'how many?' if his suit is the same length.

Non-dealer continues with either:
a 'a point of... I score...,' restating his point and its score;
b 'good' conceding the point; or
c if the dealer had asked 'how many?' he states the face value of his point, to which the dealer replies:
a 'good' conceding the point;
b 'not good...,' stating the face value of his point if greater and claiming the point score; or
c 'equal' if the face value is the same. In this case, neither player scores.
The player who wins the point always ends by saying: 'A point of.... I score...,' giving the point value and its score.

Declaring a sequence

Non-dealer: 'A sequence of...,' stating the number of cards in his longest one.
The dealer replies with either 'Good,' 'Not good' or 'How high?' and the dialogue continues as for points. The reply to 'How high?' is to name the top card of the sequence.

Declaring a meld

The non-dealer begins by declaring 'A three (or a fourteen) of...,' stating the denomination of his meld. The reply can only be 'Good' or 'Not good' as players cannot have equal melds.

A sample declaration

The declaration of points, sequences and melds follow each other.
Non-dealer: 'A point of four.'
Dealer: 'Good.'

Non-dealer: 'A point of four. I score four. A quint (sequence of five).'
Dealer: 'How high?'
Non-dealer: 'Jack.'
Dealer: 'Not good. Queen. Also a tierce (a sequence of three). I score eight.'
Non-dealer: 'A trio of queens (three queens).'
Dealer: 'Not good. A quatorze (fourteen in kings). I score fourteen. I start with 22.'
Non-dealer: 'I start with five.' He scored four for his point plus one for leading the first trick (see Scoring tricks).

A sample of English-style declaration

The dealer only declares his combinations after the non-dealer has led the first trick.
Non-dealer: 'A point of four.'
Dealer: 'Good.'
Non-dealer: 'A point of four. I score four. A sequence of five.'
Dealer: 'How high?'
Non-dealer: 'Jack.'
Dealer: 'Not good.'
Non-dealer: 'A trio of queens.'
Dealer: 'Not good.'
The non-dealer then plays the leading card to the first trick, saying: 'I start with five.'
The dealer then makes his declarations: 'A quart to queen, also a tierce. Eight. A quatorze of kings. Fourteen. I start with 22.'

Showing combinations

It is sometimes ruled that all the winning combinations must be shown before they are scored.

However, it is standard practice for a player to request his opponent to show his combination, which is immediately replaced in the hand. If an opponent does not request a show, none is given.

Playing

The first trick is led by the non-dealer. Players must follow suit if possible. If not, any card may be discarded. The player winning the trick leads to the next one.

Scoring tricks

a For leading to a trick: 1 point
b For taking a trick led by the opponent: 1 point
c For taking the last trick: 1 point
d For taking seven or more tricks: 10 points

Every time a player scores, he records it and announces his running total.

There are some optional variations to scoring for tricks:
1 a player only scores for leading to a trick if the leading card is 10 or higher;
2 a player only scores for winning a trick if the winning card is 10 or higher.

Scoring additional points

a Carte blanche (a hand with no court cards at the deal): 10 points
b Pique (a score of 30 points by the non-dealer before the dealer scores anything): 30 bonus points
c Repique (a score of 30 points by either player before the lead to the first trick): 60 bonus points
d Capot (taking all 12 tricks during play): 40 bonus points

The player cannot also claim the 10 points for taking seven or more tricks (see Scoring tricks).

Scoring the partie (game)

1 The scores for each deal are added together to give players their individual total. If a partie consists of six games, six totals will be added. Some people prefer a partie of four games. In this case the scores for the first and the last deals are doubled before the four totals are added.

2 If both players have reached or exceeded the rubicon (100 points), the winner is the player with the higher total.

The winner's score then becomes the difference between his and his opponent's totals, plus a bonus of 100 points for winning the partie.

3 If one or both players have totals of fewer than 100 points, the player with the lower total is 'rubiconed'. The other player is the winner and his score then becomes the sum of his and his opponent's totals, plus a bonus of 100 points for winning the partie.

Sample scores

	totals	**final score**	
dealer	120	120-108+100 = 112	winner
non-dealer	108	nil	
dealer	95	nil	
non-dealer	125	125+95+100 = 325	winner
dealer	82	nil	
non-dealer	85	85+82+100 = 267	winner

PIQUET AU CENT

This variation of piquet has a different final method of scoring. There is no fixed number of deals; instead, play continues until one player has reached 100 points. When the hand in which 100 points are reached is complete, the game ends.

The winner is the player with the higher total. His final score is the difference between his own and his opponent's totals. If his opponent's total is less than 50, the winner doubles his final score.

AUCTION PIQUET

This version concentrates on the playing of the hands. Players bid for tricks.

Bidding

Before the discard, the non-dealer makes a bid or passes. The dealer reshuffles and makes another deal if both players pass. When a bid has been made, bidding continues until one person passes.

The smallest bid is seven. A bid may be a plus or a minus, to win or lose the stated number of tricks. Plus and minus bids rank equally, and the highest number wins the contract, which the bidder aims to fulfil.

Doubling and redoubling

A player may say 'double' after any of his opponent's bids, indicating that he thinks he can prevent the bidder from fulfilling the bid, if it became the contract.

When a bid has been 'doubled', the bidder may call 'redouble' if he is confident he can fulfil his bid.

Both a doubled and a redoubled bid can be outbid, but if not the final score will be affected.

Differences in playing

The rules for the rest of the game are the same as for standard piquet, except as follows:

a players need not discard;

b declarations can be made in any order;

c a player may not sink (withhold a declaration) on a minus contract;

d pique is scored after 21 points in a minus contract and 29 points in a plus contract;

e repique is scored after 21 points in a minus contract and 30 points in a plus contract.

Differences in scoring

A player gains a point for every trick he takes, even if he did not lead to it.

Leading to a trick and taking the last trick do not give extra scores.

Scoring the contract

The bidding player scores 10 points for every trick he wins (on plus contracts) or loses (on minus contracts) that are in excess of his contract.

A player's opponent scores 10 points for every trick the bidder fails to make (on a plus) or lose (on a minus) to fulfil his contract.

Scoring doubling and redoubling

If the bidder fails to fulfil a doubled contract, he doubles the score for tricks made above his bid on a plus contract and for extra tricks lost on a minus contract. These are both called overtricks.

If the bidder fails to fulfil a doubled contract, his opponent gains double the score on the tricks the bidder failed to make (on a plus contract) or failed to lose (on a minus contract). These are called undertricks.

If a contract has been redoubled, then the doubled scores for overtricks and undertricks, as described for a doubled contract, are doubled.

Scoring the partie

The bonus for the partie is 150 points; rubicon is 150 points.

Rummy

Internationally one of the most popular card games, rummy evolved from rum poker, which was played in 19th-century saloons in the USA.

Players

Any number from two to six, each person playing for himself.

Cards

The standard deck of 52 cards is used and ace ranks low. J, Q and K of each suit are worth 10 points each; all other cards are face value, with ace worth one point. Melds are made by:

a grouping three or four cards of the same rank; or

b making a sequence of three or more cards of the same suit.

Melds

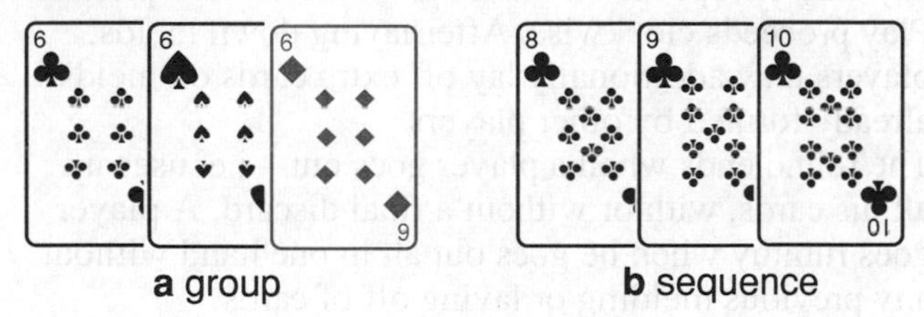

a group **b** sequence

Aim

Individuals try to be first to go out by melding all their cards.

Preparing

The first dealer is chosen by low cut. He then shuffles the cards and invites the player on his right to cut the pack. A winning score is agreed (see Scoring) and scores are kept on paper.

Dealing

Cards are dealt singly in clockwise rotation, the number depending on how many players there are:

a two players are each dealt 10 cards;

b three to four players are each dealt 7 cards;

c five to six players are each dealt 6 cards. A stock is made by turning the pile of undealt cards face down. A discard pile is begun by turning up the top card from the stock and placing this upcard on the table, next to the stock.

Playing

The player to the left of the dealer begins by choosing to take either the upcard or the top card from the stock. He may then lay face up on the table any meld he holds. Finally, a card must be discarded. This can be any card except the one taken from the discard pile.

Play proceeds clockwise. After laying down melds, players may additionally lay off extra cards on melds already formed by other players.

The round ends when a player goes out – i.e. uses up all his cards, with or without a final discard. A player goes rummy when he goes out all in one hand without any previous melding or laying off of cards.

If no player has gone out before the stock is used up, a new stock is made by turning the discard pile face down, without shuffling.

After a player has gone out, there is a new deal for the next round. The deal passes clockwise from the first dealer.

Scoring

When a player goes out, his score is the combined numerical value of all his opponents' cards in hand. When a player goes rummy, the score is doubled.

Winning the game

The first player to reach the agreed score wins the match.

GIN RUMMY

A simple, fast, two-handed variation of rummy. The rules are the same as for rummy except as described here.

Cards

Two standard decks of cards are used, one being dealt while the other is being shuffled by another player in readiness for the next round. The cards rank normally with ace low.

Rank

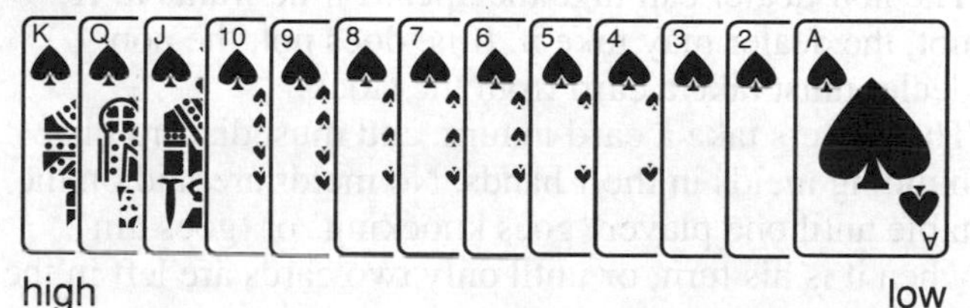

Players

Standard gin rummy is for two players. It can be played by any number of people, by dividing the players into two sides. Pairs can then play against each other simultaneously.

Aim

Each player tries to meld all his cards, but a player can still win under certain circumstances even when he does not meld all his cards.

Preparing

Pencil and paper should be to hand for scoring.

Players agree to one of the following:

a the number of rounds to be played;

b a maximum score; or

c a time limit on the match.

Dealing

The person cutting the higher card can choose which deck to use, where to sit and if he wants to deal.

Beginning with his opponent, he deals 10 cards each, singly and face down. The 21st card is turned up and this upcard starts the discard pile. The other cards are placed face down to form the stock pile.

Playing

The non-dealer can take the upcard if he wants it. If not, the dealer may take it. If he does not, the non-dealer must take a card from the stock.

The players take a card in turn, and must discard one, building melds in their hands. No melds are laid on the table until one player 'goes knocking' or 'goes gin' when it is his turn, or until only two cards are left in the stock.

Ending the round

a Going gin happens when a player melds all 10 cards.

b Knocking is an option when the value of unmelded cards totals 10 or less. To knock, a player draws a card at his turn, knocks on the table and throws away one card. Melds and unmelded cards are laid down. The other player then puts down his cards and can lay off any of his unmelded cards on the opponent's melds.

c A tie is declared and a new hand dealt by the same dealer when two cards remain in the stock and the last player cannot go gin or knock. No points are scored. When the round is over, a line is drawn under or around the score of the player winning that hand. This is called a box.

Scoring points

Scores for each hand and a running total are kept for each player. Points can be gained in four ways:

1 a gin gains 25 points plus the value of the loser's unmelded cards;

2 a player who knocks gets the difference in value between the unmelded cards of the two players unless his opponent has an unmelded card count equal, to or greater than his. Then the opponent gets the points plus a bonus of 25 points;

3 every box (winning hand) nets 25 points;

4 a bonus of 100 points is gained by the player to first reach 100 points in a game.

Sample of scoring sheet for one game

hand	player A score total	player B score total
1st	11 – 11	0 – 0
2nd	0 – 11	0 – 5
3rd	19 – 30	0 – 5
4th	0 – 30	0 – 32
5th	25 – 55	0 – 32
6th	21 – 76	0 – 32
7th	45 – 121	0 – 32
total	121	32
game bonus	100	
boxes	125	50
total score	346	84

Whist

Whist became popular when Edmond Hoyle described it in the first published rule book of card games in 1746. It was a refinement of the older game of triumph, sometimes called whisk. Whist has since spawned many challenging games such as solo whist and contract bridge.

Players

Four people play in pairs. Partners sit opposite each other.

Cards

The standard deck of 52 is used. Ace ranks high. A set of four cards, one played in turn from each player, is a trick.

Aim

Partners cooperate to win tricks.

Preparing

The first dealer is chosen by high cut for which ace ranks low. Any player can shuffle the cards before the dealer makes the final shuffle and invites the player on his right to cut the pack.

Dealing

The whole pack is dealt in clockwise direction. Cards are dealt singly, face down, except the last one which is turned up to assign trumps for that hand. The dealer claims this card when he makes his first play.

There is a misdeal if any player receives fewer or more than 13 cards or if any but the last card is revealed. Players can agree to proceed after mistakes are corrected, or a redeal can be claimed before the first trick is played. The redeal passes to the next player clockwise.

Playing
The first player to the left of the dealer leads the play by laying a card face up in the middle of the table.
Each person in turn plays one card of the leading suit face up. Anyone who cannot follow suit may use a trump or any other card.
The trick is won by the person playing:
a the highest trump card; or
b the highest ranking card of the leading suit.

Sample tricks
a leading suit clubs

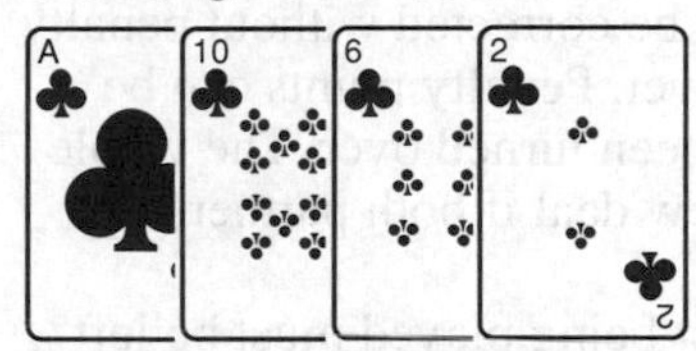

ace clubs takes the trick

8 clubs takes the trick

b leading suit hearts, diamonds trumps

2 diamonds takes the trick

The winner claims the trick by turning it face down in front of him, and leads play for the next trick. The game continues until the hand of 13 tricks has been completed.

If all 13 tricks are won by one partnership, it is called a slam.

Subsequent deals for each new hand pass clockwise to the next player, who shuffles as before. A new trump suit is declared at each deal.

Conventions

a A revoke is caused by not playing the leading suit when able to do so. It may be corrected without penalty before the trick is turned over. Penalty points can be demanded if the trick has been turned over. The whole hand is abandoned for a new deal if both partnerships revoke.

b A card exposed when not being played must be left face up on the table. The opposition then call at their discretion for it to be played during the hand. It may not be used to make a revoke.

Common techniques include:

a finessing by playing the third highest of a suit when also holding the highest;

b leading with a trump when holding five or more;

c leading the fourth best of the longest suit;

d showing that ace is held by leading K; and

e playing low as second player and high as third player.

Scoring game points

Game points can be won from tricks, honour cards and penalties. Partnerships keep a record of the number of tricks made in each hand. The first six tricks do not score. Tricks seven to thirteen score one game point each, for example:

Tricks in each hand:	6	7	2	10	8	4	etc.
Game points from hand:	0	1	0	4	2	0	

From this stage onwards scoring systems differ. The two most common are described here.

The seven-point game is used in America. In addition to points from tricks, partners who revoke give the opposition two game points. The final score for each game is the difference between seven and the losers' total. The final hand, after seven points have been reached, is usually played out and the additional points added to the final score.

The five-point game is used in English whist. In addition to points from the seventh trick upwards, there are points from honours, revokes and winning games.

a Four points are gained by partnerships holding all four honour cards, which are ace, K, Q and J of trumps. Two points are gained by holding any three honour cards.

Trick points take precedence over honour points if both partnerships reach a score of five points in the same deal. At the end of the game, the losers' honour points, if any, are discounted.

b Revokes attract three penalty points, allotted according to one of the following alternative rulings which must be agreed for the whole match:

i three points are lost by the revoking couple;
ii three points are gained by their opposition; or
iii three points are transferred from the revokers to the opposition.

c A game is declared when a partnership gains five points. The hand may be played out for additional points. The winners of the game get three extra points if opponents have a nil score; two if opponents have one or two points; and one if opponents have three or four points.

Winning the match

Three games make a rubber. If the first two games are won by the same partnership, the third game is not played. The partnership winning two games gets two extra points towards their final score.

The match is won by the partnership with the highest points total at the end of a rubber.

Beggar My Neighbour

An exciting, easy game for two to six players in which winning depends largely on luck.

Cards

For two or three players, a standard deck of cards. It does not matter if a few cards are missing. Four or more players need approximately two packs.

Aim

To win all the cards in an agreed time limit.

Dealing

All the cards are dealt out one at a time; the deal might not be even. Nobody is allowed to look at their cards, which each player collects in a face-down pile.

Playing

The person on the dealer's left begins by placing his top card face up in the centre of the table. In turn, clockwise, each player adds a card to the centre pile until someone turns up an ace, J, Q or K (court card). The player so doing demands payment from the next player as follows:

a for an ace:	four cards
b for a K:	three cards
c for a Q:	two cards
d for a J:	one card

The payment cards are turned over and put on the central pile.

If a payment card is an ace or a court card, the next player has to pay the correct number of cards. This continues until payment is complete without aces or court cards. Then the last player who turned up a court card or ace takes the whole pile and adds it under his own. He then starts the next round with the next card in his pile.

Winning the game

The winner is the player who first goes out by using up all his cards. If nobody has gone out at the end of the time limit, the winner is the player with fewest cards.

Payments

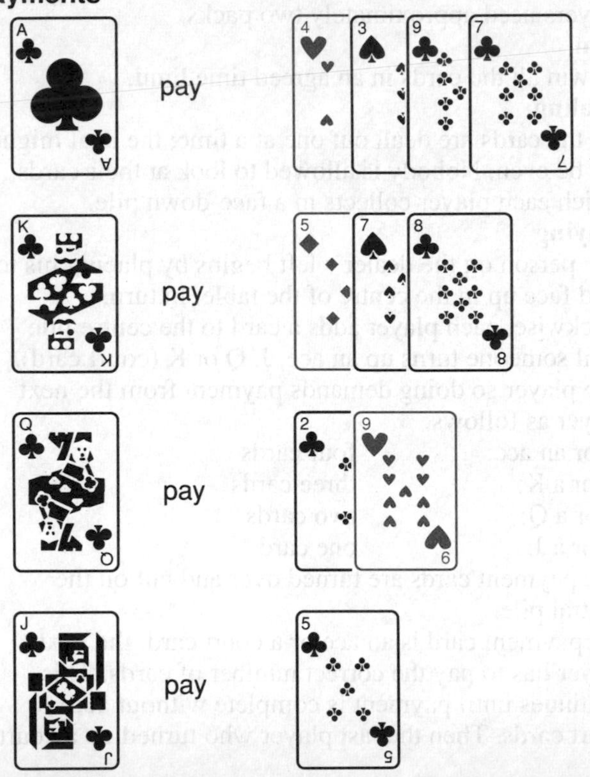

Card Dominoes

A game of skill and chance for two or more players, also known as sevens, fan-tan or parliament.

Aim

Each person tries to be the first to add his cards in sequence to a layout on the table.

Dealing

All 52 cards in a standard deck are dealt one at a time, face down, to each player in clockwise order.

Playing

Players sort their own cards into sequences in each suit. Whoever holds the 7 of diamonds begins play by putting it face up on the table. In turn, clockwise, players add a diamond card in sequence:

a going up from 7 through 8, 9, 10, J, Q, K; or

b going down from 7 through 6, 5, 4, 3, 2, ace.

A player can add a card to a sequence or start a new sequence with another 7. If he cannot do either, he passes and the turn goes to the next player.

Winning the game

The first player to use up all his cards is the winner but the game goes on until everyone has played their cards and completed the four sequences.

Example of play in progress

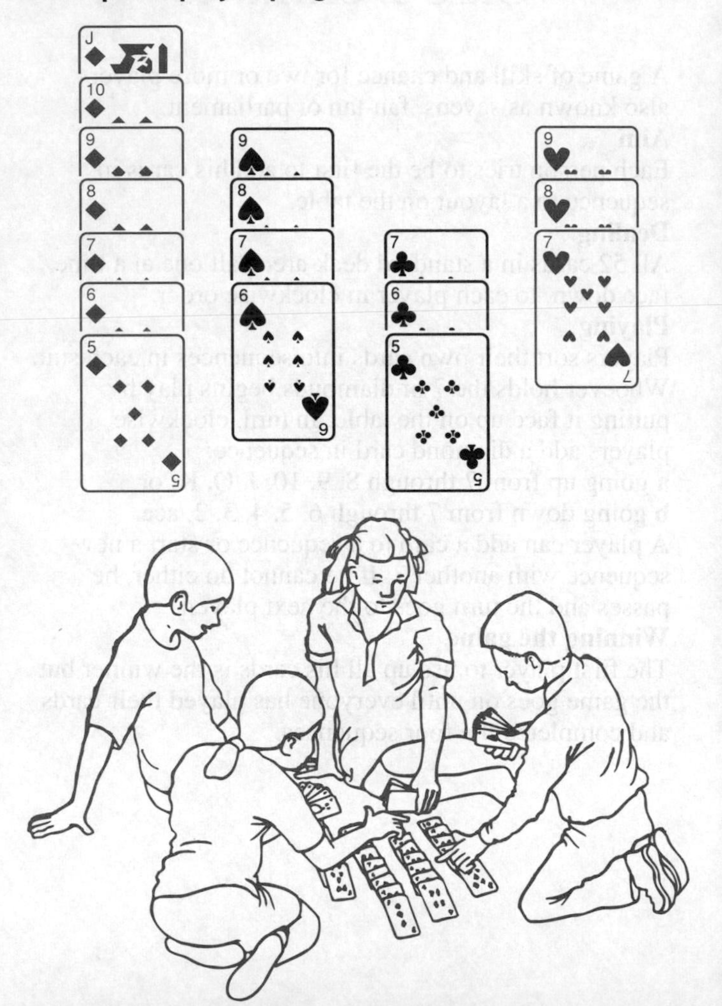

Cheat

A game for people who love risks and calling others' bluffs. Sometimes known as 'I doubt it', cheat is fun with many players but can be played by as few as three.

Aim

Everyone tries to be first to use up their cards.

Dealing

One or two standard decks of cards are used and all the cards are dealt. The hands might be unequal.

Playing

After sorting his cards, the player to the left of the dealer puts one to four cards, supposedly of the same rank, face down on the table in a pile. At the same time he calls out their rank – e.g. 'three 6s'. If he is cheating, the cards will not be what he calls.

The players, in turn, play or pretend to play one to four cards of the next higher rank.

Cheating

This can be done in two ways:

a by putting down cards other than the ones he calls (a player who cannot follow with the next higher rank will have to pretend); or

b by putting down more cards than he calls.

Calling someone's bluff

Anyone can challenge a player suspected of cheating by calling, 'cheat' or 'I doubt it' before the next player covers the cards.

When challenged, a player must turn up the cards he played. If he was cheating, he has to pick up all the cards played so far, but if he was not cheating, then the challenger must pick them up. Whoever picks up the pile starts the next round.

Winning the game

The winner is the person who manages to play his last card without being challenged or his last card is covered by the next player's cards before anyone challenges.

UP-AND-DOWN CHEAT

Up-and-down cheat is a variation that allows players to discard cards of the same or a lower rank than the previous player's.

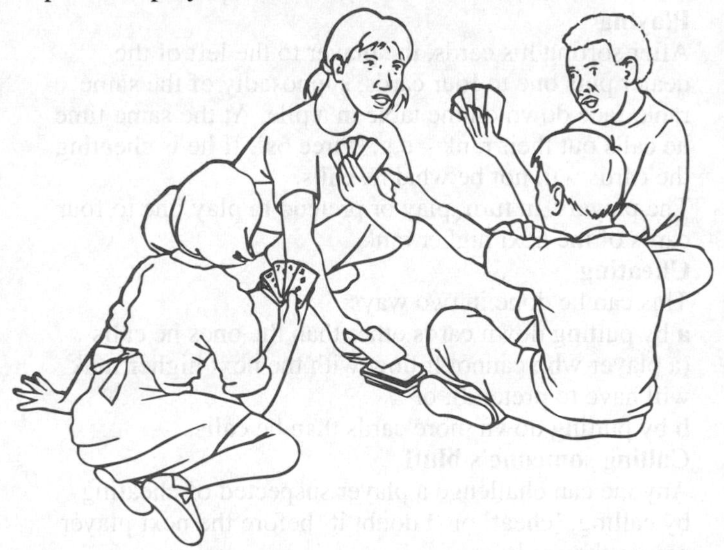

Donkey

A fast-moving, noisy game for three or more players. Penalties are the letters of the word 'donkey'.

Aim

Each player tries to avoid losing six rounds of the game and consequently becoming the donkey.

Cards

Although 'donkey' cards can be purchased, a standard pack is frequently used.

A set is four cards with the same number or picture. The number of sets needed is the same as the number of players. For example, the aces, Ks, Qs, Js and 10s of each suit would make the five sets needed for five players.

The cards are well shuffled and dealt out so that each player has four mixed cards.

Objects

Buttons, spoons or other non-breakables are needed. One fewer objects than there are players are placed in the middle before each round.

Playing

Everyone puts one card he does not want face down on the table and slides it to the player on his left. Everyone looks at the new card and decides whether to pass that card on or change it for one from his hand before passing it on.

This goes on very quickly until one player has a set of four cards of the same value (four 10s, four Qs etc.). This player quietly puts the set face down on the table and picks up one of the objects. Immediately everyone else tries to get an object. The one who fails loses and gets the D of donkey on the score sheet.

Donkey

The game is lost by the player who loses six rounds of the game and collects all the letters of donkey. His penalty is to 'hee-haw' for the other players.

PIG

This game is played the same way as donkey but without objects. Instead, the first player to collect a set of four cards puts his finger to his nose. The last player to do so becomes pig for that round. The first player to lose 10 rounds is called prize pig, loses the game and must say 'oink oink'.

Fish

A game of chance and skill for two, but better with more players. A standard deck of cards is used. A happy families pack may be preferred by younger players.

Aim

Players try to get rid of all their cards.

Dealing

If two or three are playing, each is dealt seven cards; if four or five, each gets five cards. The remaining cards are placed face down to form the stock, or fish pile.

Playing

Players sort their own cards into groups of the same rank (number or picture), keeping them hidden from the others.

The person on the left of the dealer asks anyone for cards of the same rank as one he holds. For example, if he holds the 6 of hearts in his hand he might say, 'John, give me your 6s.'

If 'John' has any, he must give them to the asker. The asker can then ask someone else for cards either of the same rank as the first or a different rank, as long as he holds one such card in his hand. He can go on asking for cards until a player does not have the card he wants.

A player who does not have a card of the requested rank tells the asker to 'fish'. The person told to fish takes one card from the fish pile, and the person who said 'fish' continues the game by becoming the asker.

Anyone who collects all four cards in a set puts them face down in front of him.

Winning the game

The winner is the first person to have no cards left except a collection of sets. If two people run out of cards together, the one with the most sets wins.

Sets are four cards of the same rank

Give Away

An easy game for two or more players who enjoy speed and alertness. A standard deck of cards is used.

Aim

Players try to be first to get rid of their cards.

Dealing

All the cards are dealt out, one at a time and face down, without anyone seeing them. The cards stay face down in a pile in front of each player. An unequal number of cards in each hand does not matter.

Playing

The player on the dealer's left turns his top card over. If it is an ace, he places it in the middle of the table and turns another card over. If it is 2 of the same suit, he adds it to the ace.

When a card is neither an ace nor a card that can be added to any other face-up card, going up or down in sequence, it is placed next to the player's own pile and the turn passes to the next person clockwise.

Sequences are built in rank order ace, 2, 3, 4, 5, 6, 7, 8, 9, 10, J, Q, K. Cards can be added to the centre or to any player's pile of upturned cards.

If a player's last card goes onto his own upturn pile, he waits until his next turn to turn the pile over, face down, and start again taking from the top.

If his last card goes into the centre or onto another's pile, the player can immediately turn his pile over and continue to play.

The winner is the one who is the first to discard all his

cards either onto the centre pile or another player's upturn pile.

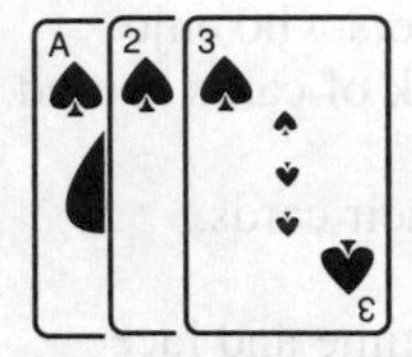

Play to centre

Play to own or other's face-up card

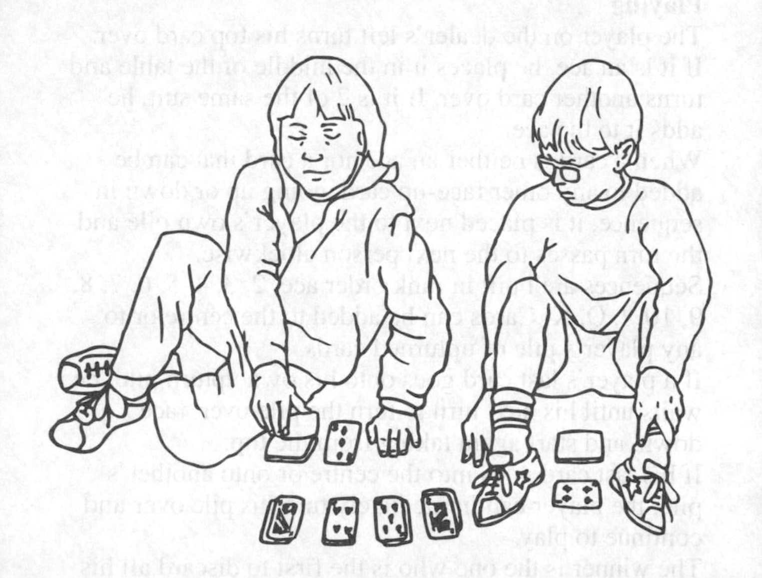

Go Boom

A simple game for two or more players, which very young children can also enjoy. A standard deck of cards is used in which ace ranks high.

Aim

Everyone tries to get rid of all his cards first.

Dealing

Players cut; highest cut deals seven cards, one at a time, to each player clockwise.

The remaining cards are put face down in the centre of the table.

Playing

All players sort their cards and the person to the dealer's left starts the round by placing one of his cards face up on the table.

The next player, clockwise, adds a card that is:

a the same suit (all hearts etc.); or

b the same rank (number or picture) as the one before.

When a player cannot follow with one of the above, he picks cards from the spare pile until he gets a card he can play.

When everyone has played in that round, the person who played the highest ranking card starts the next round. If there is a tie, the one who played first starts the next round.

When the spare pile runs out, a player has to say 'pass' and it is the next player's turn.

Winning the game

The first to get rid of all his cards is the winner. He proclaims this by shouting 'boom'.

SCORING GO BOOM

A variation in which points are scored for going boom, making the game more complex. The player who goes boom scores points for all the cards still held by the other players, as follows:

a K, Q and J: 10 points each
b ace: 1 point each
c all other cards: face value

The winner is the person first to score a number of points that has been agreed, usually 250 points.

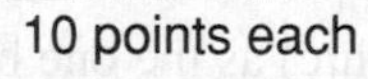

10 points each 1 point

CRAZY EIGHTS

This variation is played like go boom but using the 8s as wild cards which can be played on any card. The player of an 8 chooses which suit follows it.

The player who goes boom scores points for all the cards still held by the other players, as follows:

a 8: 50 points each
b K, Q, J: 10 points each
c ace: 1 point each
d all other cards: face value

If the spare pile runs out before anyone goes boom, each player counts the value of his cards in hand and the winner is the one with the lowest total. The winner then scores the difference between his own total and the combined totals of the other players.

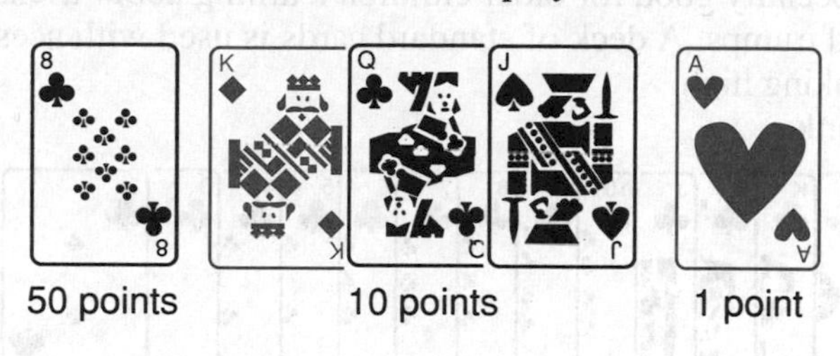

Knockout Whist

A simple form of whist for two to seven players, especially good for older children learning about tricks and trumps. A deck of standard cards is used with aces ranking high.

Rank

Aim

Everyone aims to win all the tricks of a hand and to avoid being eliminated from the game.

Trump suit

At each deal one suit becomes the trump suit; cards of that suit beat those of other suits.

Tricks

A trick is a group of cards, one played by each person in turn. The suit of the first card played to a trick is called the leading suit. The trick is won by the highest card of the leading suit.

The highest cards are aces, then Ks, Qs, Js, 10s and so on down to 3s and 2s.

If the leading suit is not the trump suit, a trump card takes the trick.

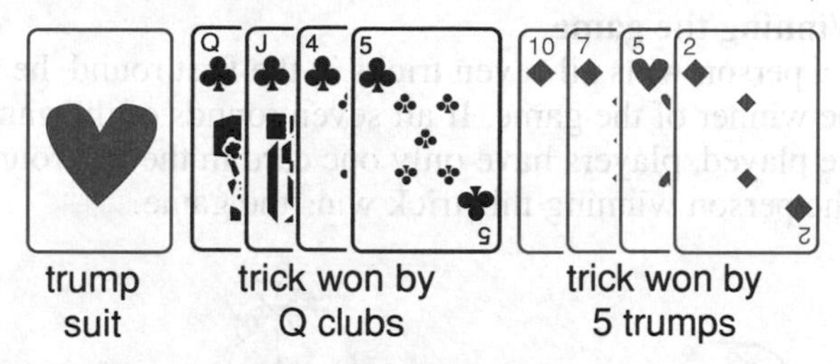

Some tricks made by four players

Dealing

Clockwise, one person deals each player seven cards, one at a time and face down. The rest of the cards are piled face down in the centre of the table and the top card turned over. The suit of this card is trumps for that deal.

At each new deal players' hands have one fewer card.

Playing

Players sort their cards into suits in rank order. The player on the left of the dealer plays one card face up to start the first trick. The other players in turn add a card, following suit. If they cannot, they may use a trump card or play any other card.

The trick is won by the person who:

a plays the highest trump card; or

b by the highest card of the leading suit if trumps are not used.

The winning player starts the next trick.

Play continues until all seven tricks have been made. Anyone who has not won a trick then drops out. The person winning the most tricks in the round begins the next round.

Winning the game

If a person wins all seven tricks in the first round, he is the winner of the game. If all seven rounds of the game are played, players have only one card in the last round. The person winning this trick wins the game.

Memory

Also known as pelmanism or concentration, this is a simple game of observation and memory for any number of players.

Aim

Everyone tries to collect as many cards as he can.

Cards

One standard deck of cards is needed for two or three players; two decks woud be better for more players. The cards should be fairly new and clean so they look alike from the back and do not give away clues about their identity by being torn or creased. A large flat area is needed for playing, such as the floor or a large table.

Dealing

One person shuffles the cards and places them all face down and separate, so they are not touching.

Playing

The player on the dealer's left turns over any two cards so that all players can see them.

If they are the same rank, such as two Ks or two 5s, he keeps them and turns over two more cards.

The player continues in this way until the two cards do not match. Then he leaves them exactly where they were, face down. The next player clockwise then has a turn.

If a player turns a card up the same rank as one that has already been turned and replaced, he must try to remember where it was, hoping to make a pair.

Play continues until all the cards have been taken. The player with the most cards is the winner.

Menagerie

Also called animals, this game is for two or more players, the more the better. It is great fun and very noisy. Two standard decks of cards are used.

Aim

Each player tries to win all the cards.

Choosing animals

Each player chooses an animal name that is long and hard to say. These names are written on small pieces of paper, which are folded and shaken up together in a hat or box. Each player takes one and has that animal for the game. Everyone then learns the names of all the animals.

Dealing

All the cards are dealt clockwise, one at a time and face down. The hands might be unequal. A player must not look at his cards but put them in a face-down pile.

Playing

The player on the left of the dealer turns his top card over to begin his face-up pile. Each does the same in turn.

When a player notices that another face-up card is the same rank (same number or picture) as his face-up card, he must shout out the name of the other player's animal three times.

The first player to correctly shout out wins the other player's face-up pile, adding them to the bottom of his own face-down pile.

If a player calls the wrong name, he must give all his face-up cards to the player whose name he shouted.

A player wins when he has collected all the cards.

My Ship Sails

Easy to learn, this game is exciting when played at high speed. It is for four to seven players using one standard deck of cards, ace ranking high.

Aim

Players try to collect seven cards from the same suit, such as seven hearts.

Dealing

The dealer is the person who cuts the highest card. Seven cards are dealt to each player, one at a time and face down, clockwise. The rest of the deck is not needed.

Playing

Players sort their cards by suits. They decide which suit to collect, although these can change as cards are exchanged.

Exchanging

Each person puts an unwanted card face down on the table and slides it to the player on the right, who picks it up. Each then discards another card, slides it to the right and picks up his own new card from the left. This continues until one player's hand is all one suit and he shouts 'My ship sails'. The first to do so is the winner.

My ship sails

Old Maid

An easy game for three or more young children, also called 'pass the lady'.

Aim

There are no winners. Instead, players try to avoid being the loser by getting rid of all their cards.

Cards

A standard deck of 52 cards is used with one of the Qs removed. This leaves a deck with a pair of Qs in one colour and a single Q – the old maid – in the other.

Old maid

one Q removed

old maid

pair of Qs

Dealing

All the cards are dealt, face down and one at a time. Hands might be unequal.

Playing

Players sort their cards, keeping them hidden from other players. Anyone holding pairs of matching cards puts them out face up. Pairs are two cards with the same number or picture.

If someone holds three matching cards, he only puts down one pair and keeps the odd card. If he has four, he puts down two pairs.

The player to the left of the dealer spreads his cards in his hand, keeping them hidden. He offers them to the player on his left who takes one card. If the card matches one already held, he puts down the pair. If not, he puts it in his hand, and he in turn spreads his cards for the player on his left.

The game continues in the same way until all the cards have been put down in pairs except the old maid, which cannot be paired. The person holding the card is called 'old maid' by the others and loses the game.

VARIATIONS

The French game is called le vieux garçon (old boy), which is the J of spades. All the other Js are removed from the deck.

Another version requires pairs to be matched for colour as well as number, such as a pair of red aces or a pair of black 10s.

Le vieux garçon

three Js removed

J of spades is the old boy

Pairs

Play or Pay

A game using rank and sequence for three or more players. It is also called round the corner.

Aim

Players try to win counters by getting rid of their cards in each round.

Dealing

Each deal is one round of the game. Players should agree how many rounds will make the game.

One player deals all the cards clockwise from a standard deck, one at a time and face down. Players might not have equal numbers.

Each player also starts with 20 counters.

Playing

The player on the dealer's left plays one card face up.

The next player, on his left, looks to see if he can follow that card with one in the same suit in sequence: ace, 2, 3, 4, 5, 6, 7, 8, 9, 10, J, Q, K.

If the card played is the K, the sequence goes 'round the corner' to the ace of that suit.

If a player holds the next card in sequence, he plays it face up on top of the last card. If he does not, he must pay one counter into the middle of the table.

The person playing the last card of a suit then plays any card from his hand to start the next one.

Winning the game

The winner of the round is the first person to play all his cards. He takes all the counters from the centre.

Losers each pay him one counter for every card they still hold.

The winner of the game is the person with the most counters after the agreed number of rounds.

Cards in sequence

Racing Demon

A noisy game for any number that is played at great speed and requires a lot of space.

Aim

Players try to use all 13 cards in their piles and play as many cards as they can into the middle.

Cards

Each player needs a complete deck of 52 cards. Old cards with different backs are the best.

Dealing

Players shuffle their own decks and deal themselves 13 cards face down. The pile is turned up and four more cards are dealt face up side by side with it. Players keep their remaining cards face down in one hand.

Playing

One person is the starter who shouts 'go' to start the game once everyone has dealt. Players put cards into the centre or on their own row of four cards as fast as they can.

Playing into the centre

If a player has an ace, this should be put face up in the centre. The 2 of the same suit, followed by the 3, 4, 5, 6, 7, 8, 9, 10, J, Q, K in that order, can then be played by the person holding them.

Playing onto the four face-up cards

Each player can play onto his own row of four cards but must play in descending order, alternating black and red cards. For example, red K, black Q, or black 9, red 8, black 7 and so on.

Which cards can be played

a The top card from the 13 pile.

b A card or a sequence of cards from one of any other face-up piles. Gaps made by doing this are filled with the top card from the pile of 13.

c If neither of the above is possible, the player turns three cards over from the spare pile in his hand to make a new face-up pile. This is continued until the player gets a card he can play. When the spare pile runs out, the face-up pile is turned over to use as a spare pile.

Ending the game

A player shouts 'out' as soon as he has used up all the cards from his original pile of 13.

Scoring

The cards from the centre are sorted into their different decks. Each player counts how many cards are left in his original face-up piles. His final score is this number subtracted from the number from his deck in the centre. The player with the highest score is the winner.

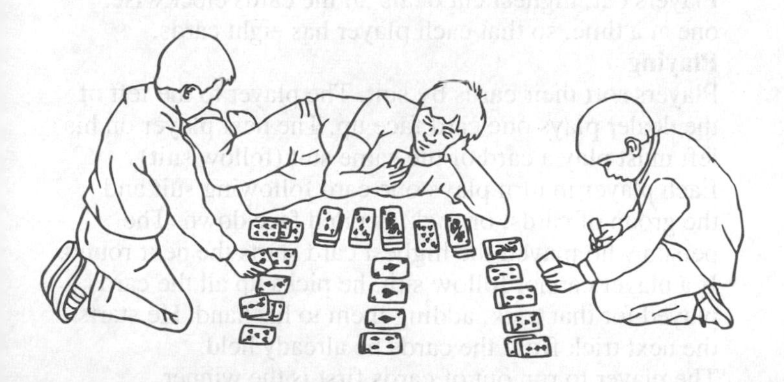

Rolling Stone

A popular game with unexpected moments for four, five or six players.

Aim

Players try to get rid of their cards.

Cards

One standard deck is used with the 2s removed for six players; 2s, 3s and 4s removed for five; and 2s, 3s, 4s, 5s, and 6s, removed for four. Ace ranks high.

Rank

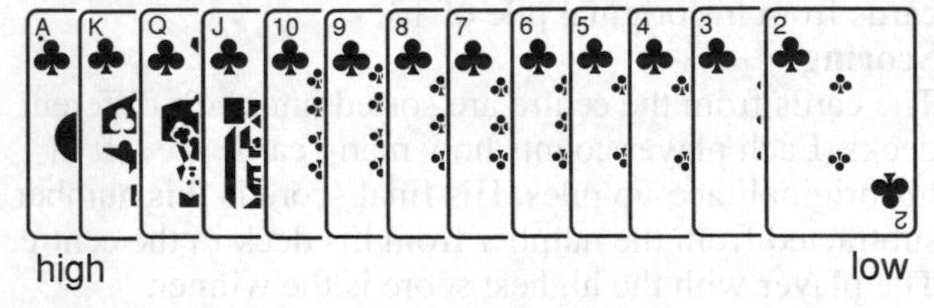

Dealing

Players cut; highest cut deals all the cards clockwise, one at a time, so that each player has eight cards.

Playing

Players sort their cards by suit. The player to the left of the dealer plays one card face up. The next player on his left must play a card of the same suit (follow suit). Each player in turn plays one card following suit and the group of cards, or trick, is piled face down. The person who played the highest card starts the next round. If a player cannot follow suit, he picks up all the cards played for that trick, adding them to his hand. He starts the next trick from the cards he already held.
The player to run out of cards first is the winner.

Slap Jack

An easy, exciting game for two or more players, and very good for young children.

Aim

Everyone tries to win all the cards. The game can be played with or without a time limit.

Cards

A deck of standard cards is used. Two decks can be mixed if more than three play, and if some cards are missing it is not important.

Dealing

The whole deck is dealt by one person, face down and one at a time in clockwise direction. Players must not look at their cards, which they put in piles in front of them. Some might have more than others.

Playing

The player to the left of the dealer turns his top card over and places it face up in the centre. Then the player to his left does the same.

Play continues like this until someone plays a J. Then every player tries to be first to put his hand on it and 'slap the jack'. The one who does so gets the whole pile of cards, shuffles them with his own and piles them face down to use. The player to his left starts the next round.

If two people slap the J, the winner is the one with his hand underneath.

If someone loses all his cards, he has one chance to stay in the game by being the first to slap the J on the next round. If he fails, he must drop out of the game.

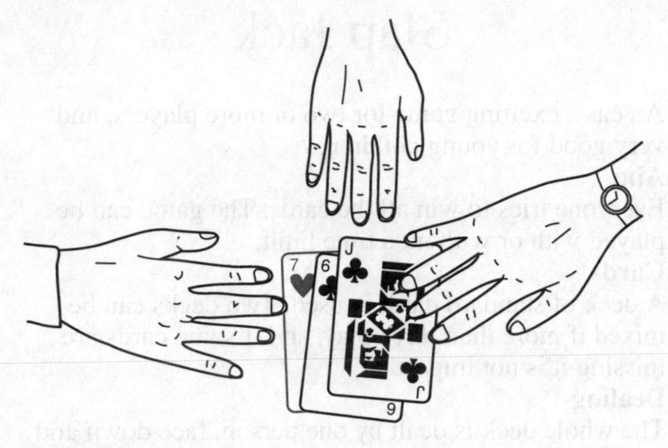

Penalty
When someone slaps the wrong card, he must give his next card to the player whose card he slapped.
Winning the game
The game is won when:
a a player collects all the cards; or
b a player holds the most cards at the end of an agreed time limit.

Snap

A very popular, noisy game of great fun for two or more players.

Aim

Everyone tries to take all the cards.

Cards

An old, standard deck is fun to use, although special snap cards are available. Two decks are better for more than three players. If some are missing, it does not matter.

Dealing

All the cards are dealt out by one player, singly and face down in a clockwise direction. Players do not look at their cards. It does not matter if some players have more than others. Everyone piles their cards in front of them, face down.

Playing

The player on the left of the dealer turns his top card over and puts it face down next to his own pile. The next player on his left does the same, making another upturned pile of his own. All the other players do the same in turn. When a player runs out of face-down cards he turns his face-up pile down and continues.

Snap

When one player sees that the cards on top of two piles match, such as two 8s or two Ks, he shouts 'snap!' The first to do so collects both the piles which have the matched cards and adds them to the bottom of his own face-down pile.

Play continues with the person to the left of the last person to turn over a card.

Snap

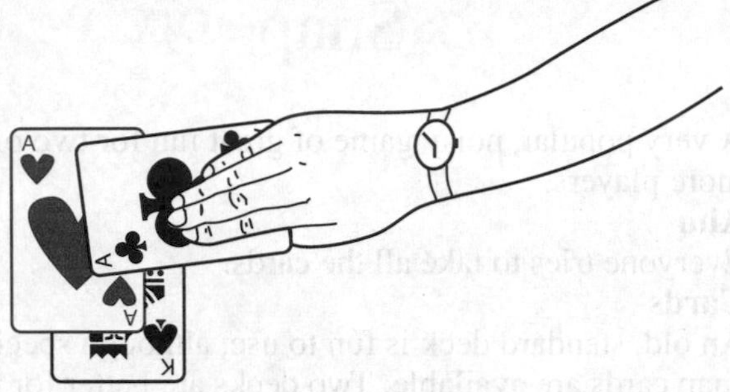

The snap pool

When two players shout snap at the same time, the two piles of cards are placed together in the centre and are called the snap pool.

Play continues as before. When someone turns up a card that matches the card on top of the pool, he shouts 'snap pool!' and takes the whole pool.

Penalty

Everyone should agree which penalty is to be paid when a player incorrectly calls snap:

a) the player pays each person one card from his face-down pile; or

b) the player's face-down pile is turned over, placed in the centre and becomes a snap pool.

The winner is the one player left with cards.

EASY SNAP

Very good for young children, this variation has only one, central face-up pile. Snap is shouted when the top two cards match.

SPEED SNAP

This version is very fast-moving because everyone turns their cards over at the same time instead of in turn.

Snip-snap-snorem

A fast, hilarious game for three or more players using a standard deck of cards.

Aim

Everyone tries to get rid of his cards.

Dealing

Players cut; highest cut is thc dealer. Ace is high in this game.

All the cards are dealt one at a time, face down and clockwise. Some players may have more than others.

Playing

Players sort their cards, putting together cards that match each other in order, such as two 4s, a 5, four 6s, one 7, two 10s, three Js and so on.

The player to the left of the dealer plays one card face up in the centre.

If the next player to the left has a card that matches, he puts it down and shouts 'snip!' If he has another matching card he must wait for his next turn to play it. If he cannot play a card he says 'pass'.

Play continues in turn, clockwise, until a player puts the third matching card in the centre. He shouts 'snap!' The player to put down the fourth matching card shouts 'snorem!' He then starts the next round.

Winning the game

The first player to get rid of all his cards is the winner.

VARIATION

When a player has two or more matching cards, he plays them all together, shouting 'snip snap' or 'snip snap snorem'.

Sample play

JIG

This is played the same as snip snap snorem, but players put down sequences of four cards which can be from different suits, for example 5, 6, 7, 8. The players shout 'jiggety, joggety, jig!' when they play each card.

Stealing Bundles

Also called stealing the old man's bundle, this game is for two to four players using one standard deck of cards. Young children able to match cards of the same rank will enjoy it.

Aim

Players try to collect the most cards.

Dealing

One player deals each player four cards, singly and face down in a clockwise direction. The next four cards are then put face up in a row in the centre. The rest of the deck is put face down to one side.

Playing

The player to the left of the dealer looks to see if he has a card that matches in rank one in the centre. If he has, he captures the centre card and puts it face up with his own near him. This is his 'bundle'.

If a player's card is the same rank as two or three centre cards, he can capture them all at the same time.

If a player's card is the same rank as the top card in somebody's bundle, he can capture the whole bundle.

If none of a player's cards matches any centre card he must 'trail', or put one of his own cards face up in the centre.

Everyone plays a card in turn. Whenever cards are captured, they are put on the bundle with the matching card face up.

Cards of the same rank

Extra deals

When everyone has played all of his four cards, four more cards are dealt to each player, and none to the centre, and the game continues.

Winning the game

When all the cards have been dealt and played, the player with the most cards in his bundle wins.

War

An easy introduction to card playing, war is for two players using a standard deck of cards. It can be varied for three players.

Aim

Everyone tries to get all the cards.

Dealing

One person deals the whole deck one at a time face down. Both players put their cards face down in a pile without looking at them.

Playing

Each player turns over the top card of his pile and puts it in the centre face up next to the other player's card. The player whose card is the higher ranking, regardless of suit, collects both cards and adds them to the bottom of his pile.

Players continue to turn over cards together and collect them.

Rank of cards in mixed suits

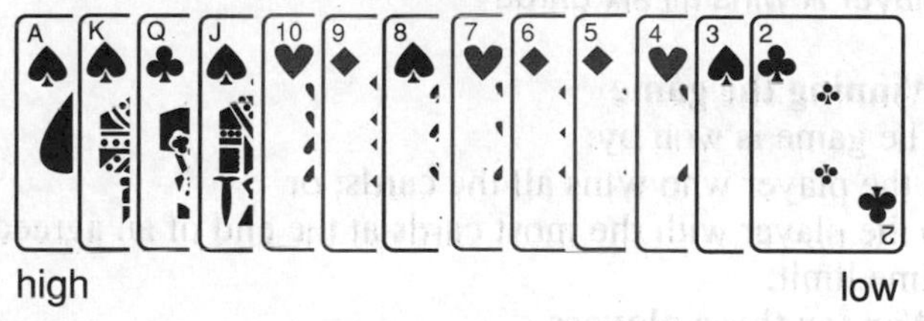

War

War occurs when two cards of the same rank are turned over.

Both players then put another card on top of their first

card, but face down, and another face up. The higher ranking of the last two cards wins all six cards.
If these are the same rank, the war continues, and the player turning up the higher ranking card will claim 10 or more cards from the centre.

Playing war

player A

player A wins all six cards

Winning the game

The game is won by:

a the player who wins all the cards; or

b the player with the most cards at the end of an agreed time limit.

War for three players

Played as for two players except:

a the last card is not dealt out, so all players have the same number;

b when any two cards of the same rank are turned over, all three people play war;
c when all three turned-up cards are the same rank, everyone plays double war;
d when playing double war everyone puts two cards face down to one card face up, and if the cards match they continue with single war.

PERSIAN PASHA

In this variation, players turn over their top cards and begin a face-up pile next to their face-down pile. Both players turn over cards until they have a match, when the player of the higher-ranking card wins the other's entire face-up pile.

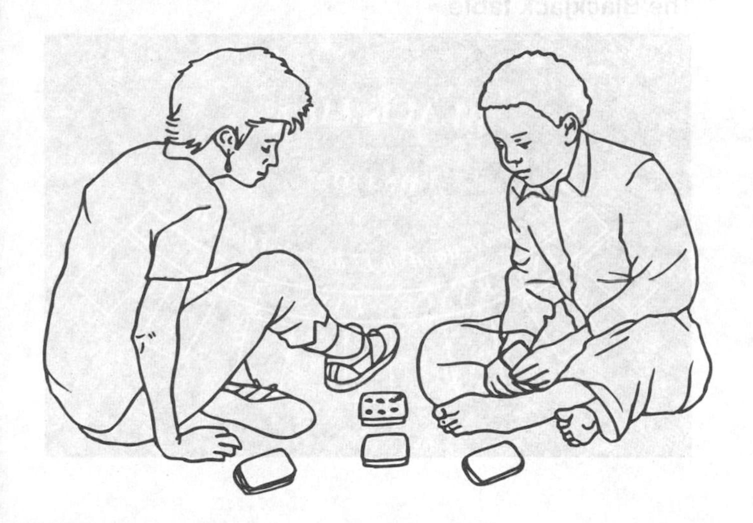

Blackjack

Also called 21, this game is usually for two to six or seven active players.
In European casinos, other people, known as 'kibitzers', may 'piggyback' by standing behind an active player, placing bets on his or her hand.
There can be any number of kibitzers. They may not advise any player how to play.

The Blackjack table

A regulation table, upon which the game will be played, is marked with seven places.

The Blackjack table

Other equipment

In addition to the regulation table, the following special equipment is needed:

1 four standard 52-card decks, shuffled together, making one deck of 208 cards;
2 a rack of betting chips;
3 a box for dealing cards, known as the shoe;
4 a box for receiving discards;
5 two jokers, known as 'indicator cards'.

Points value of the cards

Each card has a points value. Ks, Qs and Js count as 10. An ace counts as 1 or 11 at the discretion of the player who holds an ace. The value of a dealer's ace is fixed at 1 or 11 by the house rules and remains constant. In the description of play given here, the dealer's ace is counted as 11.

All other cards (2s to 10s) count at their face value. Because there are four packs of cards in the deck, there will be sixteen of each rank of card, e.g. sixteen aces; four aces of each suit.

Aim

Each player tries to make a higher card count than the dealer, aiming to reach 21 points but going no higher.

Betting limits

Each casino sets its own maximum and minimum limits, which must be announced to the players.

Shuffling and cutting

The dealer shuffles the cards and hands one of the indicator cards to any player, saying 'Cut please.'

The player pushes the indicator card into the deck where he or she wants it cut.
The dealer cuts the deck, putting the indicator card and all the cards in the cut above it underneath the remaining cards, i.e. the indicator is at the bottom of the deck.

The cut

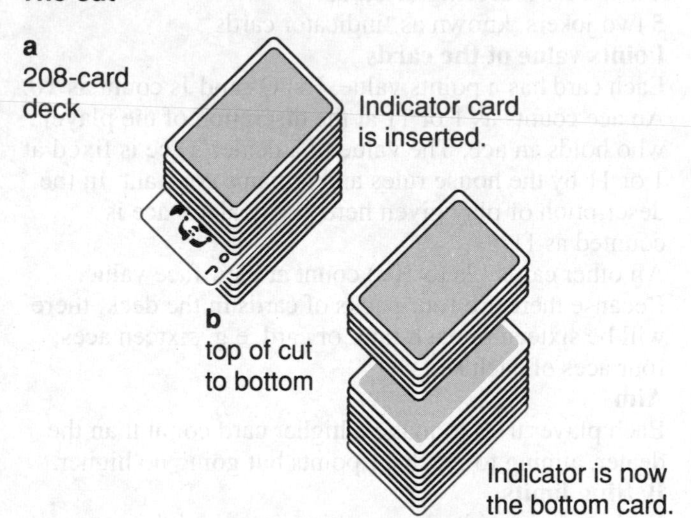

The second indicator
The dealer places the second indicator card about 50 cards above the bottom one and puts all the cards face down into the dealing shoe.
The top card from the shoe is then discarded.
The cards are now ready for dealing, which will be done after the betting takes place.

The dealing shoe

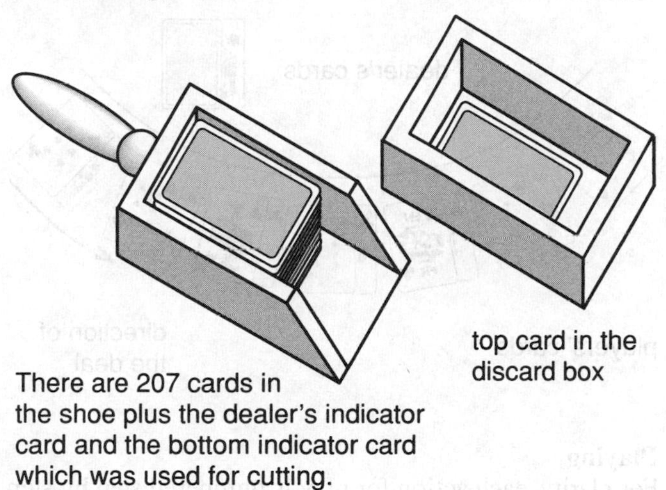

There are 207 cards in the shoe plus the dealer's indicator card and the bottom indicator card which was used for cutting.

Betting

Players bet any amount between the limits by each placing chips on the betting space directly in front of them.

A player may bet on several hands, if there are betting spaces available, but must play to completion the hand on his or her far right before playing the next hand, and so on.

Dealing

When betting is complete, the dealer begins with the player on the left and deals one card face up to everyone, in clockwise order, and lastly to him- or herself. The dealer repeats this process, but deals his or her own second card face down.

The completed deal

Playing

For clarity, each action for play is numbered step by step, but some steps will be omitted in actual play according to how the cards come out in the deal.

Step one

Players add up the total value of their two cards.

Any player making a card count of 22 or more is immediately 'busted' and loses the bet to the banker, who sweeps it up instantly.

The losing player's two cards are disposed of in the discard box.

Step two

If the dealer's face-up card is a 10 or an ace, he or she looks at the face-down card.

If it is a 'natural 21' (two cards totalling 21 exactly) the dealer places it face up on the table and calls 'blackjack'.

If any other players have a natural 21, they also call and

that hand is declared a stand-off by the dealer. No chips are paid or collected by players who have natural 21s in a stand-off. All other players not having a natural 21 lose to the dealer, who collects their bets.

The natural 21

any ace plus any 10, J, Q or K

Step three

If the dealer does not have a natural 21, play continues, beginning with the player on the dealer's far left.
If the player has a natural 21, he or she says 'blackjack' and the dealer pays that player the winnings. The player's cards are then placed in the discard.

The winning odds

The dealer's odds are fixed at 3 to 2. This means that for every two units the player has bet, he or she wins three units and collects five, i.e. the original stake of two plus the three units won.

Step four

If the two cards dealt to each player do not total 21, each must choose one of two options:
a to stay with the cards dealt because another card might cause a bust by taking the count over 21. The player says 'I stand' and slips the cards under the bet; or

b to draw a card in the hope of improving the count.
The player says 'hit me' or beckons to the dealer who deals a third card, face up, next to the player's original pair.
Players may draw as many cards as they like, one at a time, until they stay by calling 'I stand.'
If the count goes over 21 during the draw, the player goes bust and loses the bet.
If the count reaches exactly 21, the player automatically stays.

Step five

The dealer then passes clockwise to the next player, and so on round the table and back to him- or herself.

The dealer's play

If all the players go bust, the dealer puts his or her own cards into the discard and starts a new deal.
If some active players remain, the dealer turns both of his or her cards face up and plays them.
The dealer's options are determined, as follows, by the rules, marked on the Blackjack table:
1 If the count on two cards is 17 or more, up to 20, the dealer must stay.
2 If the count is 16 or less, the dealer must draw cards until the count reaches 17 or more.

The settlement

Beginning with the player on the right and moving anti-clockwise around the table, the dealer finally pays off players who have a higher count than he or she has with an amount equalling the bet they placed, and collects the placed bets from players whose count is lower.
If a player has the same count as the dealer, it is called

a stand-off and neither the player nor the dealer wins or loses; the player keeps the original bet.

Sample of the cards at the end of play

Four active players

player 1

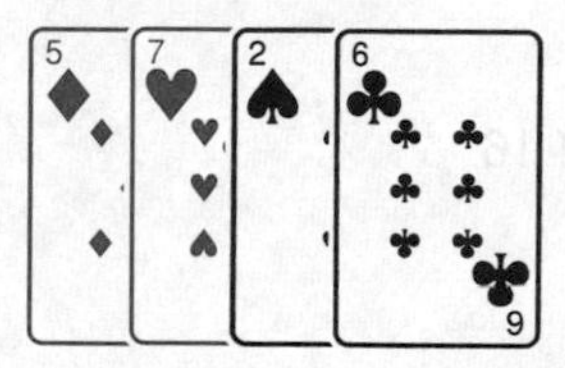

has drawn and stands with a count of 20

player 2

stands with a count of 19

player 3

(opts to score ace as 1)
draws and stands with a count of 20

Sample of the cards at the end of play (continued)
player 4

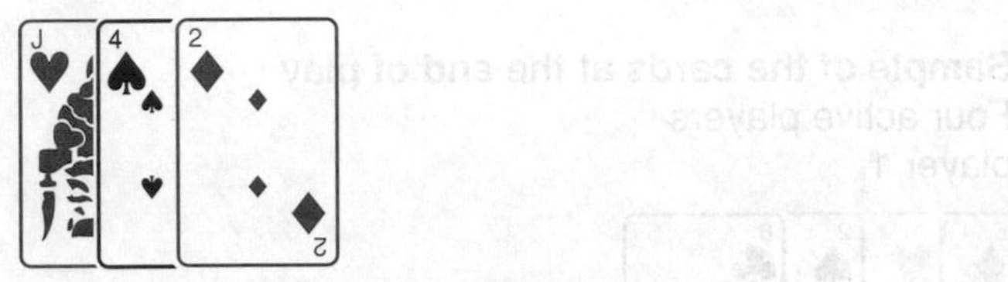

draws and stands with a count of 16

dealer

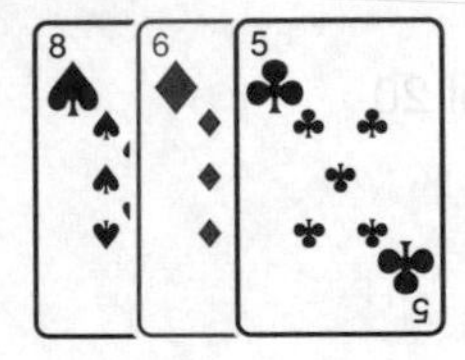

has to draw (because the pair counts 14) and stands at 19

The settlements of this sample will be as follows:

player 1:	a win, beating the dealer's count
player 2:	a stand-off, equalling the dealer's count
player 3:	a win, beating the dealer's count
player 4:	a loss, beaten by the dealer's count

As each settlement is made, the dealer scoops up the cards into the discard box.

The next round

In this round, players place their bets again and the dealer makes a new deal from the shoe.

Further shuffling and cutting

When the cards from the shoe have been used up to where the indicator card is, the dealer completes the current deal. After that, all 208 cards are collected together again, the two indicator cards are retrieved and the shuffling and cutting process is repeated before the next deal takes place.

Optional Blackjack rules

In many casinos there are several house rules, the most common of which are insurance betting, splitting pairs and doubling down.

1 Insurance betting. When the dealer's face-up card is an ace, many casinos allow players to make an insurance bet against losing to a possible natural.

In step two, before looking at his or her face-down card, the dealer asks if anyone wants insurance.

Players can insure by adding an amount equal to half their original bet next to their hand.

The dealer then examines his or her face-down card. If it is a 10-count, the pair is a natural, and the dealer turns the card face up. The insurance bettors are paid off at 2 to 1 for every unit they bet.

If the dealer's face-down card is not a 10-count, the insurance bettors lose their insurance bets and the game continues.

2 Splitting pairs. Any two cards of the same rank, regardless of suit, can be treated as a pair. This includes any two cards with a count of 10, such as Q-10 or K-J.

If the original two cards dealt to a player are a pair, the player can split them and have a card dealt on each.

If a dealt card forms another pair, that pair can also be split, and so on.

The player must put the same bet on each of the split hands. He or she must also play those hands, in order, to completion, beginning with the one on the far right.

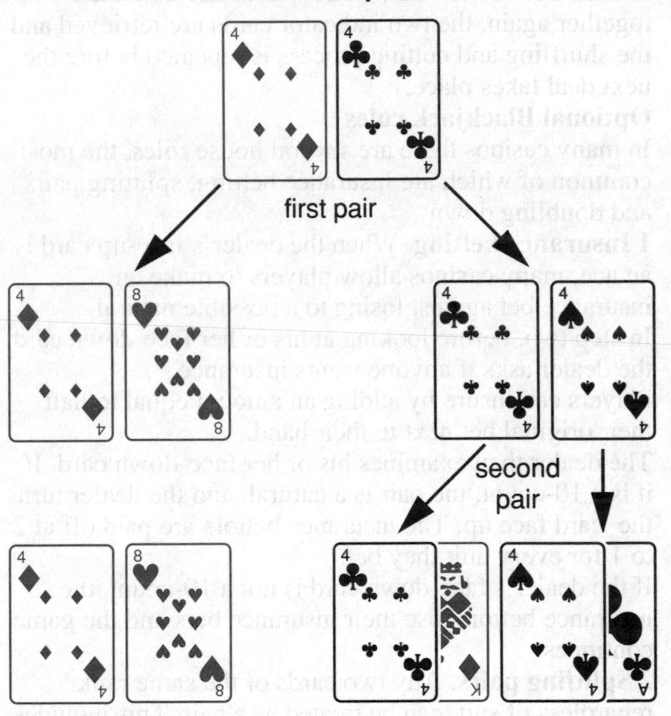

If one card of a split pair happens to make a count of 21 with the next card dealt, this does not count as a winning natural and the player is paid off at even money. No player may draw more than one card on any one of two split aces.

3 Doubling down. In some casinos, after the first two cards have been dealt, any player may decide to double the bet and have a third and final card dealt face down onto the original two.

The player may not look at this third card until the dealer turns it face up after the extra stake has been placed and the other players have had their turns.

Chemin de Fer

Chemin de Fer and its cousin Baccarat are French variations of a 15th-century Italian game. Chemin de Fer – often called Shimmy or Chemmy by American gamblers – is currently popular in European casinos; the version called Baccarat is currently more popular in the US. Though similar, Chemin de Fer and Baccarat differ in a few ways – most notably in that the casino takes no risk in Chemin de Fer.

Chemin de Fer means 'railway', a reference to the shoe (card-dealing box) which is passed from player to player as each takes a turn as the dealer.

Unlike in other banking games, when played in casinos the players in Chemin de Fer take turns as banker, playing against each other.

The minimum stake is high and the maximum is often very high.

The casino's role

The casino takes a commission on the banker's winnings, usually five percent. In exchange for this the casino provides the accommodation, the table and the services of two or three croupiers.

The croupiers

Croupiers run the game; the operating croupier supervises the shuffling, cutting and dealing of cards and also takes charge of the bankers' money, collecting their winnings and paying out their losses.

The croupiers also collect the five percent commission on winnings, which is put into the casino's money box, fitted into the centre of the table.

A Chemin de Fer table

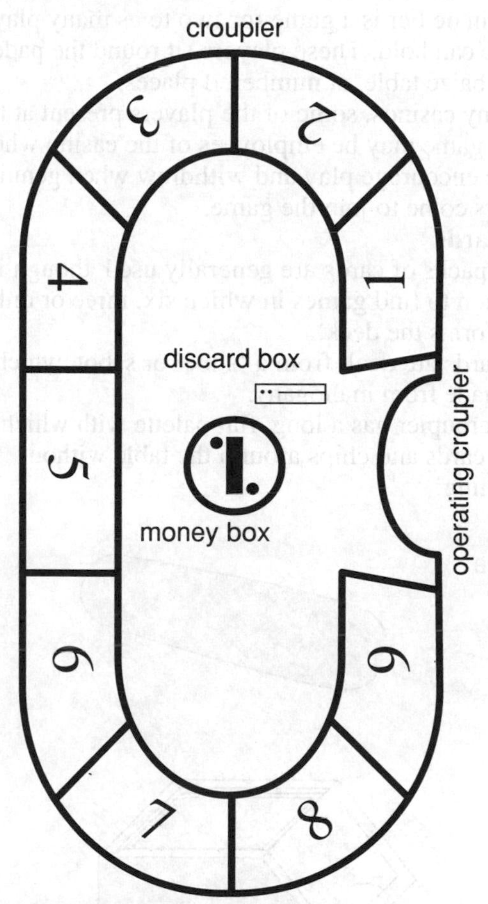

All cards going out of play are dropped into the discard box.

Players at the table

Chemin de Fer is a game for two to as many players as a table can hold. These players sit round the padded, green baize table, at numbered places.

In many casinos, some of the players present at the start of the game may be employees of the casino whose job it is to encourage play and withdraw when genuine players come to join the game.

The cards

Eight packs of cards are generally used, though it is common to find games in which six, three or only one pack forms the deck.

The cards are dealt from a 'shoe' or sabot, which is a box made from mahogany.

Each croupier has a long, flat palette with which to move cards and chips around the table without stretching.

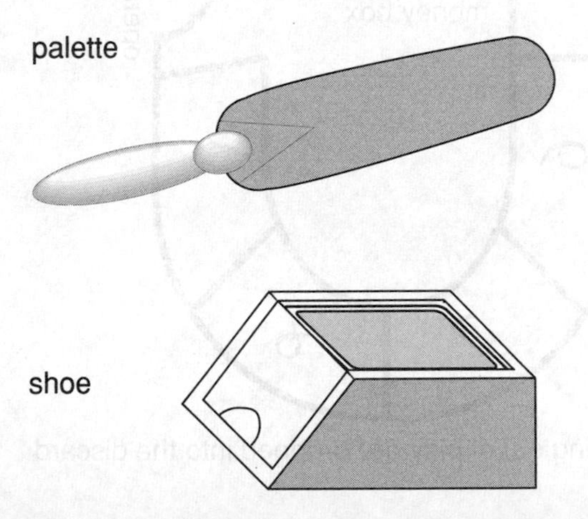

Points values of the cards
The points values of the cards are as follows:

court cards:	0 points
10s:	0 points
aces:	1 point
2s to 9s:	face value

How the points value is totalled
Units of 10 are disregarded. This means that when the total is a one-digit number, that number becomes the points value; if the total is a two-digit number, only the second digit counts, as shown in the examples.

Adding points values

cards	total	points value
10♦ 10♥ 7♠	7	7
5♣ 8♦	13	3
8♣ 6♦ 7♥	21	1

Adding points values (continued)

cards	total	points value
5 5 Q	10	0
A A A	3	3
J 5 4	9	9
6 K 6	12	2

Aim

One player, the banker, plays against one other player (known as the active player). Both aim to get a score of 9 or the closest to it. The one with the higher score wins.

If the players make the same count, new cards are dealt and nobody collects or loses.

Shuffling and cutting the cards

The following routine is followed whenever the whole deck is to be shuffled.

1 The operating croupier spreads all eight packs of cards face up on the table. It is usual to use four packs with red backs and four with blue, preferably all of the same pattern.

2 All the players and croupiers take piles of the cards and shuffle them, until all the cards have been shuffled.

3 The croupier takes the shuffled cards from each player. After shuffling them together, the croupier places them in little piles, usually seven or eight.

4 The croupier invites the players to cut as many of the piles as they wish, without exposing any card.

5 Players who want to make a cut do so one at a time beginning with the player to the croupier's right.

6 The croupier cuts any of the cards as he or she chooses.

7 Finally the croupier stacks all the cards into the shoe ready for play.

The first banker

The player sitting immediately to the right of the croupier has the option of being the first banker. If he or she doesn't want the bank, it passes to the next player anticlockwise, who may keep it or pass it on.

In some casinos there is an auction for the bank, which goes to the highest bidder. The casino collects the auction bid.

Betting

The croupier slides the shoe to the first banker who places a bet (of any amount between the house limits) on the area of the table known as the piste.

The croupier handles the banker's chips.

The banker then slides the top three cards out of the shoe and hands them to the croupier, who drops them into the discard box.

Fading

The stake placed by the banker can be equalled, but not exceeded, by bets from the other players. The process of betting is known as 'fading the bank'.

Anyone wanting to fade the bank completely, i.e. stake the same as the bank, places the bet on the piste and calls 'banco'.

If more than one player calls banco, the one sitting nearest to the right side of the banker takes precedence. This player is then known as the ponte and becomes the active player.

If nobody calls banco, players may, in anticlockwise order from the banker's right, place partial bets until the bank is completely faded. The total bets cannot exceed the banker's bet as he or she cannot pay out more than the amount staked if the bet is lost.

If the bank is not faded completely, the excess is set aside from the banker's bet, for the banker.

A bet placed on the line of the piste is worth only half its normal value and is known as a 'cheval'.

When there is no ponte, the player making the highest bet becomes the active player.

When a player calls 'banco'

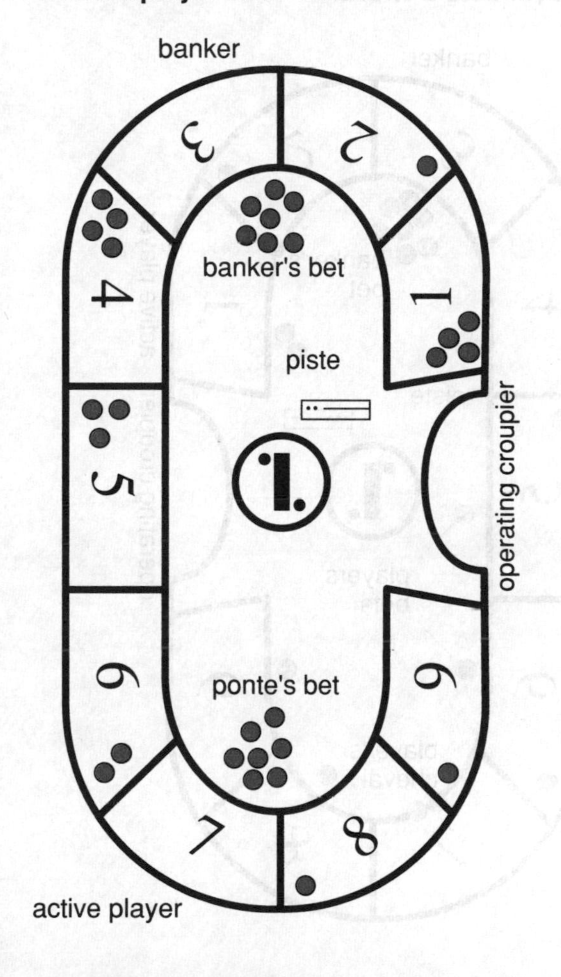

When a player bets a cheval

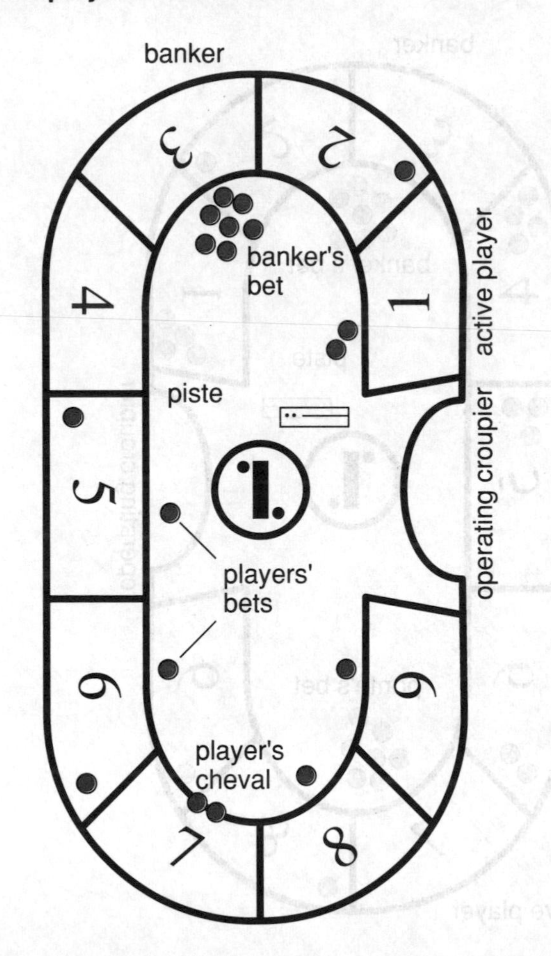

Dealing

Bankers deal by sliding one card out of the shoe and dealing it face down to the active player. They then deal one card face down to themselves, another to the active player and finally another to themselves.

Playing the first round

In this round, the active player looks at his or her dealt cards.

Situation 1. If a player's cards total 8 or 9 points, the player puts them face up on the table and the banker must show his or her cards.

Whoever has the higher score wins.

If the banker wins, the croupier collects all the bets from all the players and gives them to the banker.

If the active player wins, the croupier pays, from the banker's bet, all the players an amount equal to their original bet.

Situation 2. If at any time the active player and the banker have the same points count, their cards are discarded and the banker makes a new deal.

Situation 3. If the active player's cards total less than 8, the player calls 'pass'.

The banker then examines his or her own cards. If they total 8 or 9, the banker wins. The cards are turned face up and the banker collects the bets.

If they total less than 8, the banker calls 'pass' and the second round begins with the active player's turn again.

Playing the second and final round

In this round, the active player must draw or stay according to his or her count.

Situation 4. If the active player's count is 6 or 7, the player must stay.

Rules for the banker's second turn

Bankers must draw or stay according to these rules, unless they have an option, marked d/s, allowing them to choose whether to draw or stay.

Banker's count: Value of active player's draw	3	4	5	6	7
0	draw	stay	stay	stay	stay
1	draw	stay	stay	stay	stay
2	draw	draw	stay	stay	stay
3	draw	draw	stay	stay	stay
4	draw	draw	d/s	stay	stay
5	draw	draw	draw	stay	stay
6	draw	draw	draw	draw	stay
7	draw	draw	draw	draw	stay
8	stay	stay	stay	stay	stay
9	d/s	stay	stay	stay	stay

If the count is 5, the player has the option to stay or draw.
If the player stays, the banker must then act according to the following rules:
a if the banker's count is 6 or 7, he or she must stay;
b if the banker's count is 5 or less, he or she must draw a card from the top of the deck in the shoe.
The winner is then the one with the higher score and collects as before.
Situation 5. If the active player's count is 0, 1, 2, 3 or 4, he or she must draw a card. If it is 5, the player may choose to draw rather than stay.
The drawn card is placed face up on the table, and the banker must respond according to the table shown opposite. The banker's response depends on the count the banker holds and the value of the active player's draw card.
After the second turn is complete, whoever has the higher count wins and collects as before. A tie always invalidates the counts: the cards are discarded and a new deal takes place without any further betting.
Continuing play
Play continues in this fashion. The banker may pass the shoe of cards on to the right-hand neighbour whenever there are no bets on the table.
When the deck of cards runs out, the croupier opens new packs, which are shuffled and cut as before.

Fan Tan

Also known as Sevens, Parliament or Card Dominoes, Fan Tan requires considerable skill and is a very simple and enjoyable social and family game.

The banking version, known as Chinese Fan Tan, is a game totally based on chance, requiring no skill at all.

Players

Three to eight people can play. All players ante the pot with one chip before the cards are dealt.

Chips

In a family game it is a good idea for everyone to exchange low-value coins for large numbers of chips, as the gains and losses can be quite high, despite the skill involved.

This is an excellent game for children because they can experience the excitement, and the reality, of gambling without losing huge amounts of money.

Cards

A standard deck of 52 cards is used with aces ranking low.

Sample layout of cards in play

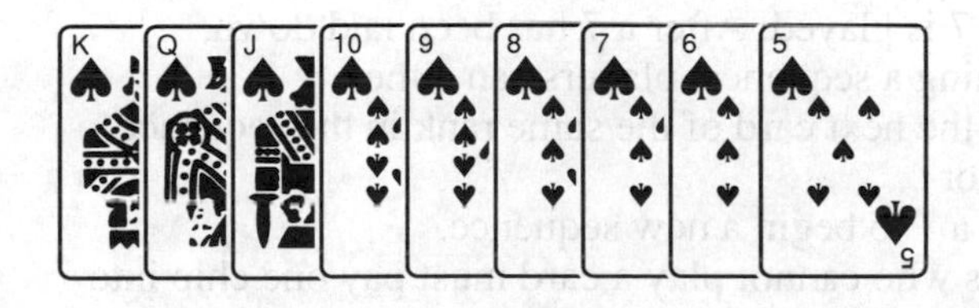

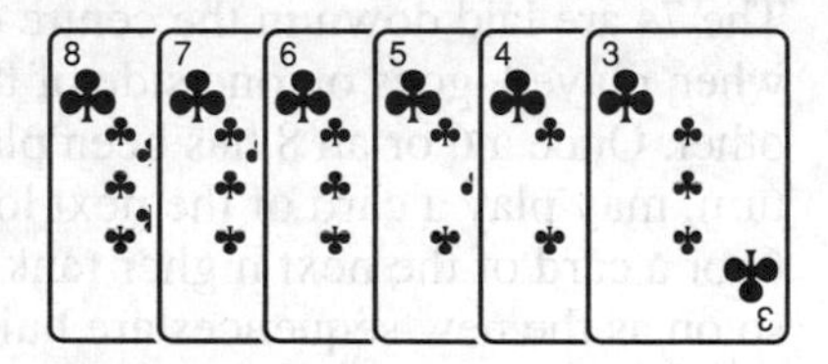

Aim

Players try to get rid of all their cards as quickly as possible.

Dealing

Players cut for who shall be the first dealer, who then shuffles and deals out all the cards, one at a time, beginning with the player to the left and going clockwise. Players deal in turn, in clockwise rotation. Because all the cards are dealt, some players may have one more card than others. Those with the advantage of one fewer card should pay another chip into the pot before play begins.

Playing

The first player to the left of the dealer begins by playing a 7, if possible. If that player cannot play a 7, the turn passes to the next player to the left, and so on until a 7 is played. After a 7 has been laid down, beginning a sequence, players can either:

a play the next card of the same rank in the sequence order; or

b play a 7 to begin a new sequence.

Players who cannot play a card must pay one chip into the pot, and the turn then passes to the next player.

The 7s are laid down in the centre of the table; a 6, when played, goes on one side of the 7, and an 8 on the other. Once a 6 or an 8 has been played, any player, in turn, may play a card of the next lower rank (a 5) on the 6, or a card of the next higher rank (a 9) on the 8, and so on as the new sequences are built.

Penalties

Players who pass when they could play must put three chips into the pot.

Those who pass when they could play a 7 must also pay five chips to players who possess the 6 and 8 of the same suit.

Winning

The game continues, the cards being played up to the K and down to the ace in each suit until someone plays his or her last card and becomes the winner.

The game then stops and everyone left holding cards puts one chip for each card they hold into the pot.

The winner then takes all the pot.

The next game can then begin with the ante as before.

Poker and variations

Poker has been given such large coverage in this section because it has so many variations and is the most popular competitive card game throughout the world, especially in the USA.
The stakes in poker can vary from a few coins to thousands of pounds. In the past, many an old prospector and his gold dust were quickly separated by skilled poker players.
Poker is a simple game. This section begins with the basic rules and is followed by the method of play for some of the more common variations.

About rules

Many rules have been invented in an attempt to guard against cheating. For the purposes of regular games among friends and family members, played in an atmosphere of mutual trust, other rules are best established by agreement over a period of time and written down. This prevents arguments and also enables new friends or colleagues, joining a regularly played game, to read the rules established earlier.

Bluffing versus cheating

The term 'poker face' aptly conveys the art of bluffing at poker. Players aim to control their facial expressions so that they don't reveal what they are thinking. The art of bluffing is an indispensable poker skill.
Cheating, however, is not an accepted part of the game, although there are people who make a profession of it. Hence it is wiser to play with the same group of friends regularly than to join in public games with strangers.

Basic Poker

The procedures explained here are the general rules for all variations of poker.

Players

The number of players can vary from two to ten.

Competition

Players win by holding the best five-card poker hand. How the cards are played is often more important than the cards a player holds. Poker is the great game of bluff.

Cards

A standard deck of 52 cards is used, with the occasional addition of one or two jokers as wild cards.

The ace ranks high except when used in any straight to count as 1 in the run.

Rank of cards

high low

Ace ranks high in a royal flush.

Ace ranks high in an indifferent hand.

This would be called an 'ace-high' hand.

Ace ranks high in tied hands.

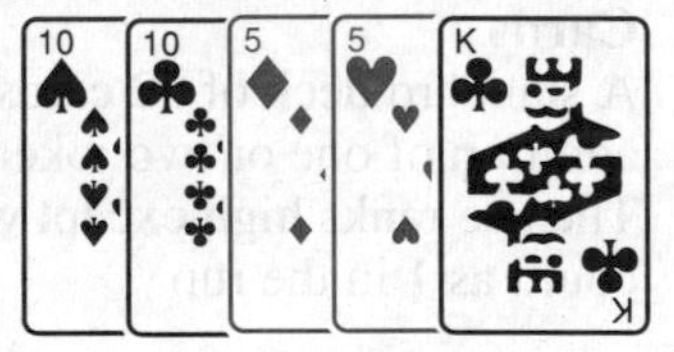

In two hands of identical pairs, the one with the higher ranking odd card wins – in this case the hand with the ace. Suits are irrelevant when ranking. This would be called an 'ace-high' hand.

Ace can rank low in a straight flush.

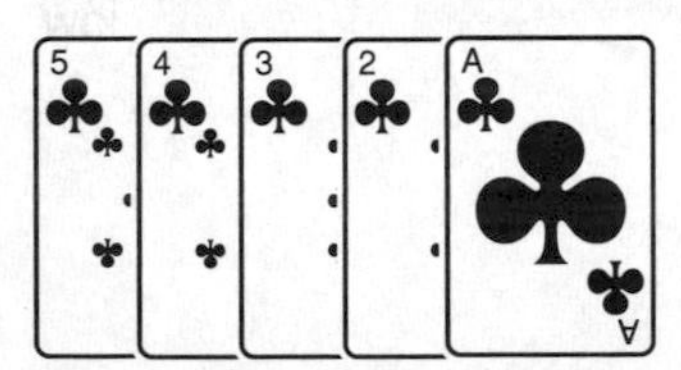

This flush would be a 'five-high' hand because ace ranks low as 1.

Use of two decks
John Scarne, one of the most authoritative voices in the world of card games, suggests that two packs of cards with different back patterns should be used.
Both decks should be thoroughly shuffled. While one is in play, the other is kept at one side to replace it whenever a player makes the request. The change would take place at the end of the current hand.
Seating
Scarne suggests that seating positions at the beginning of a game should be organized as follows:
1 one player is selected by general consensus to shuffle the cards, which are then cut by the player on the right;
2 the shuffler then deals one card face up to everyone, beginning with the player to the left and ending with the shuffler;
3 the person who has the card of highest rank chooses where to sit and becomes the first dealer for the game;
4 the other players then choose their seats, in descending rank order of their cards, from the remaining places.
Changing seats
At the end of an hour of play, any player can ask for a change of seating. The player to the dealer's left then deals for the choice of seats, as before, but also retains the deal for the next hand.
Preparing
Players should agree on the following and write down their agreements on paper:
1 exactly which version of Poker is to be played;
2 which cards, if any, shall be wild cards;
3 a time limit for the game (although everyone has the

right to leave the game at any time);
4 who will be the banker and what the value of chips is to be;
5 the maximum and minimum number of chips that can be bet at any one time;
6 a time limit for each play. Five minutes is the usual maximum allowed for a player to decide how to play. Any other active player may call 'time' when the limit is reached, and the hesitant player must drop out. That hand is then dead.

The bank

In a private, social game, players bet with small coins or have a bank and buy chips. In the latter case, one player acts as the banker, and can still take part in the game.

The banker can either be chosen by consensus or by a draw of the cards.

The banker should keep the bank's chips and cash on a separate table.

Before the game starts, the unit value of chips is agreed and players then buy chips from the bank.

At the end of the evening's play, everyone cashes in their chips.

Players can buy further supplies of chips (or can cash some in) during the game. They should do this between hands, while the table is clear.

Coloured chips

Players may decide to use coloured chips, as used in casino games. If they do, then the most common unit values are as follows:

White:	1 unit	Blue:	10 units
Red:	5 units	Yellow:	25 units

Dealing

Anyone can shuffle the cards, but the dealer has the right to make the final shuffle and offer the cut to the player on the right.

The cards are then dealt one at a time to each player in clockwise order. The number of cards dealt to each player depends on the variation being played.

If there is a misdeal, the dealer collects all the cards, shuffles and cuts them and deals again.

Aim

Players try to make the best poker hand possible.

Playing

Beginning with the player on the dealer's left, players play and bet in turn on their cards, according to the rules of the particular variation being played.

To bet, each player considers the value of his or her cards and puts a chosen stake of chips in the central pot.

When the betting is finished and players have their final hands, there is a showdown.

Winning the showdown

At the showdown, players place their cards face up on the table.

The player with the best five-card poker hand takes the pot. If there is a tie, the pot is shared.

The hands are given a rank order, with those higher up the list winning over those lower down.

A tie occurs only when the winning hands are identical.

Poker hands rank as shown on the following pages.

Standard poker hands in descending rank order

1 royal flush

Usually the top-ranking poker hand (except five of a kind, when using wild cards); the five highest cards in the same suit.

An identical royal flush would be the same run in another suit, in which case the two hands tie.

2 straight flush

A numerical sequence of five cards from the same suit.

Q-high straight flush

7-high straight flush

Q-high straight flush

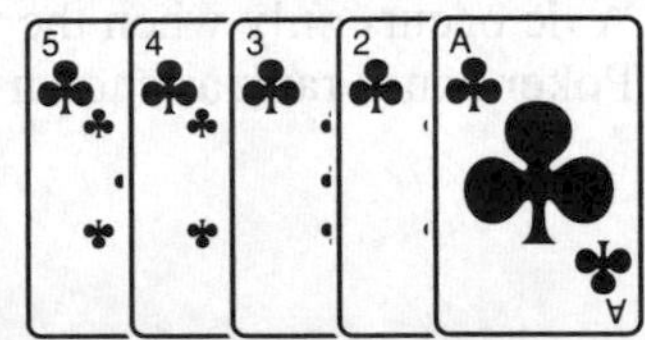

5-high straight flush

If two or more players hold straight flushes, the one whose high card ranks over the other's takes precedence.
In these four flushes, the two Q-high hands both outrank the other two and tie with each other for the winning place.

3 four of a kind

Any four cards of the same ranking.

The four Ks outrank the four deuces. The odd cards are irrelevant. Two hands of four of a kind cannot tie.

4 full house

Three cards of a kind plus another pair.

The hand with the higher ranking three of a kind wins, regardless of the rank of the pair. The full house with three 7s wins over the one with three 6s.

5 flush

Any five cards of the same suit, not in sequence.

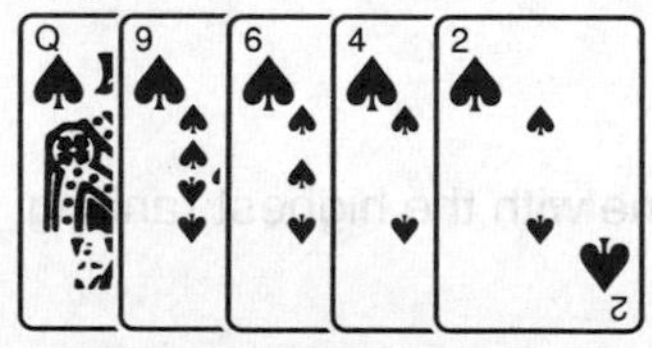

The winner, if there are two flushes, is the hand with the highest ranking card.
If both have the same top-ranking card, the player with the next highest card in rank wins, and so on. If players have identical flushes, there is a tie.

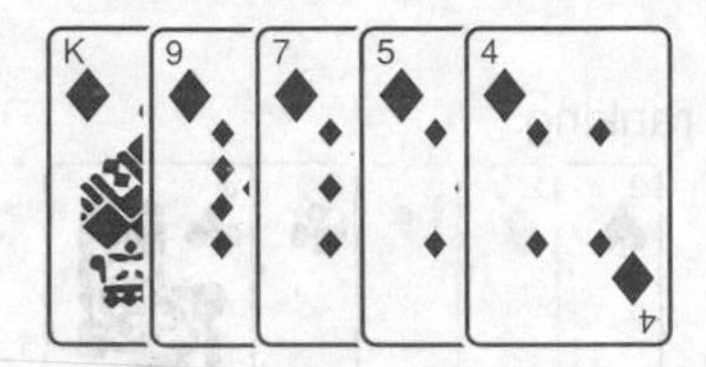

The flush with the K outranks the one with the 10, and wins.

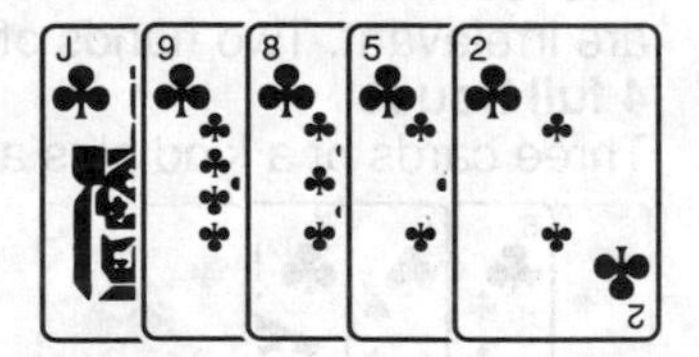

Identical flushes tie.

6 straight
A run of five cards which are not all of the same suit.

The winning straight is the one with the highest ranking card.

The J-high straight wins of these two.

Identical straights tie.

7 three of a kind

Three cards of the same rank and any two odd cards.

The winning hand is the one with the highest ranking three of a kind.

Aces rank higher than Js, so the hand with three aces wins. The odd cards are irrelevant. Two hands of three of a kind cannot tie.

8 two pairs

Two pairs of cards plus an odd (unpaired) card.

The hand with the highest ranking pair wins.

The ace pair ranks highest.

If two hands have the same highest ranking pairs, the rank of the other pair is taken into account.

The pair of 6s wins over the pair of 4s.

If both pairs match in rank, then the hand with the higher ranking odd card wins.

The 3 ranks higher than the 2.

Identical hands of two pairs tie.

9 one pair

One pair of cards of the same rank plus three odd cards.

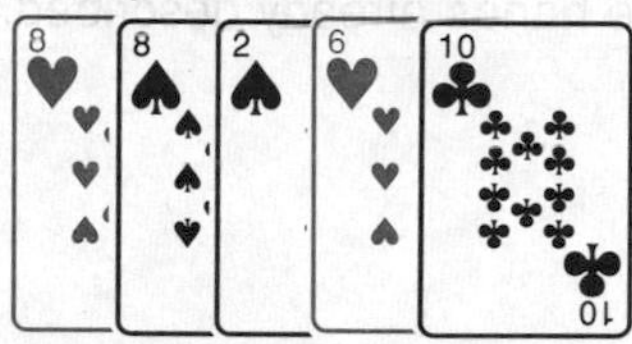

In two hands, the pair of the higher rank wins.

Ks outrank Js and win.

If the pairs are of the same rank, the highest ranking odd card wins.

The hands are identical except for one of their odd cards. Since 6 outranks 2, the hand with the 6 wins.

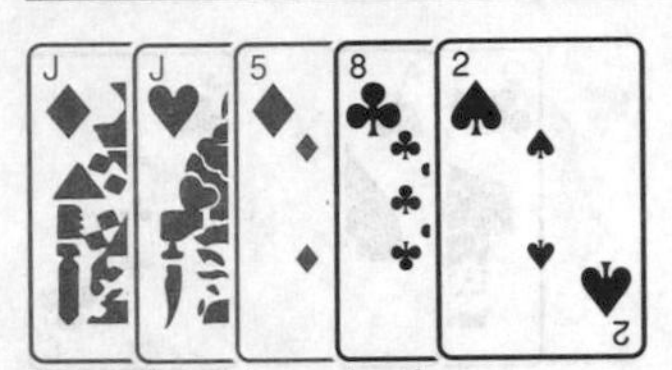

Identical hands tie.

10 high card

Any hand of five odd cards, which are neither in sequence nor make any of the hands already described.

If there are two high-card hands, the one with the highest ranking card wins.

Ace is the highest ranking card. The hand with the ace wins.

If the highest cards in two high-card hands are of the same rank, the next highest in rank among the other odd cards wins.

If all cards match by rank, the hands tie.

Use of wild cards

A wild card can be used to represent or duplicate a card of any rank and suit, including itself.

Any card or group of cards can be declared wild before a game begins.

The most common wild cards

1 one or two jokers

2 one, two or four of the deuces

3 occasionally, one, two or four of the 3s, in combination with **1** or **2** above (some are shown below)

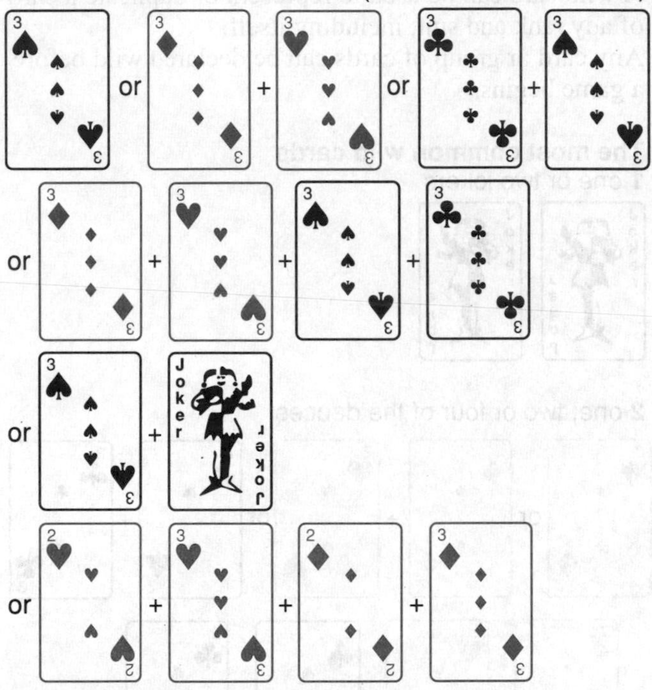

4 court cards with a design feature in common, such as one-eyed Js or Ks with moustaches

Ranking of hands using wild cards
There are two additions to the ten standard poker hands already described.

Five of a kind. This is any five cards of the same rank value, one of which will, of course, be a wild card. This hand ranks highest of all the hands, even above the royal flush.

Five of a kind in Ks

or other wild card

Double-ace flush. Ranking between full house and flush, this hand has five cards of the same suit made up of the ace, a wild card and any three other cards of the same suit as the ace.

A double-ace flush in clubs

The rank of the twelve poker hands with wild cards is as follows:

1 five of a kind (highest rank)
2 royal flush
3 straight flush
4 four of a kind
5 full house
6 double-ace flush
7 flush
8 straight
9 three of a kind
10 two pairs
11 one pair
12 high card. This is the lowest rank if nobody happens to be dealt a wild card. Since **12** cannot be made when any player has a wild card, the lowest ranking hand when wild cards are in play would be **11**.

Draw Poker

Sometimes called Closed Poker, Draw Poker has some variations of its own. It is the standard form of poker which preceded all other games.
Draw Poker is the poker most often enjoyed as a family game.

Players

Up to ten people can play, although two to six make the best game. There should be no more than six when playing for high stakes.

Cards

A standard deck of 52 cards is used. Two packs with different backs may be used alternately, whenever a player calls for a change of cards.

The pot

The centre of the table is the place where chips are placed when they are put into the pot. This enables everyone to see clearly how much is in the pot.

Aim

Players try to hold a higher ranking hand than any other player at the showdown, thus winning the pot.

Preparing

Preliminaries are the same as for Basic Poker. Players should also agree as to which type of ante and which of the stake limits they are playing during the whole game.

The ante

There are two types of ante:

1 Ante paid by all the players. Before the deal and beginning with the leader (the player to the dealer's left), each player in turn places the same amount into the pot.

2 Dealer's edge. Only the dealer antes the pot.

Optional stake limits

There are five popular betting limits.

1 A specified minimum and maximum. Examples of such limits are: a 5p to 10p limit; 10p to 25p; 10p to 50p; 25p to £1, and so on.

The ante is usually the minimum.

Each player cannot bet higher than the maximum or lower than the minimum but can bet any amount between the two.

2 Three-figure limits. In this instance limits could be: 5p, 10p and 15p. The first figure is the amount of the ante and the opening stake. After the draw, stakes must be either 10p or 15p.

The same rules apply to any three-figure limits agreed.

3 Jackpot. This is used when options **1** or **2** have been agreed but all players have passed on the first deal. Before starting the second deal, the dealer announces the amount in the pot, i.e. the total ante.

This then becomes the maximum stake that any player can make during that hand, unless it is lower than the maximum limit.

4 Pot limit. Players can stake any amount up to the total amount in the pot. If players want to raise the stakes, the pot total is calculated after adding the amount required for them to stay in the game.

5 Table stakes. This is a less popular option. Players each place whatever amount they choose on the table, above an agreed minimum. Usually there is no maximum.

Players may add to or subtract from their table stake after the showdown and before the next deal.

In turn, each player can stake up to – but not more than – the amount he or she has on the table.

A player whose table stake is less than the previous bettor has staked is allowed to play for the pot. (See **Some rules for Draw Poker: 3 Tapping out,** on p. 243.)

6 No limit. Poker with no limits to the stakes is rarely played.

Dealing

Starting with the leader and proceeding clockwise round to the dealer, players are dealt one card at a time, face down, until each has five cards.

The remaining cards are placed face down in a pile in front of the dealer. This stock will later be used for the draws.

Playing

Everyone examines their cards.

The leader begins. If holding a pair of Js or a pair of a higher rank, the leader may open the pot or pass. If not holding any such pairs, the leader must pass.

If the leader passes, the next player, seated clockwise, has the same two options, and so on.

Opening the pot

The person who makes the first stake is said to open the pot. The opener may or may not be the first player, because whoever opens the pot must hold in hand a pair of Js or a pair of a higher rank.

This rule enables players to use their skills by knowing the opener holds a high-ranking pair.

The opener places a bet in the pot, within the limits already agreed.

A player holding a pair of Js or higher is not compelled to play.

Opening the pot

Six members of the family are playing and the stake limit they have chosen is one to five chips.

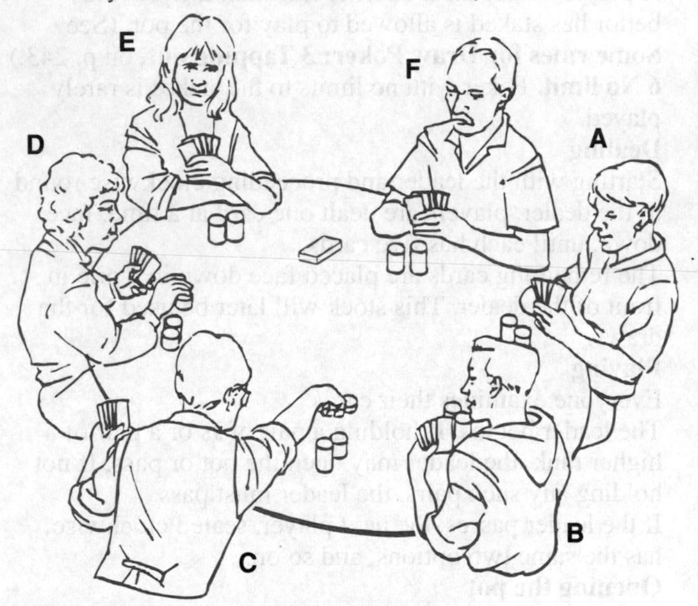

A Mum is the leader. She does not have a pair of Js. She passes.

B John cannot open. He passes.

C Dad holds a pair of Qs. He opens the pot with three chips.

D Gran can now choose to drop out, play or raise Dad's bet.

E Jill is already watching the events carefully.

F Uncle Tom is also the dealer. He will play after Jill, then Mum will have her turn again.

Splitting the opening pair
The player making the opening bet may split the pair of cards in hand, discarding one or both of the pair and keeping them to one side.
If the opener wins the showdown, he or she will have to show these cards.

Continuing play
If nobody opens the pot, because nobody holds a pair of Js or higher, then the deal ends.
Everyone antes again (unless dealer's edge is being played, in which case only the dealer antes).
The deal passes clockwise; the new dealer collects, shuffles, cuts and deals the cards again.

Play after the pot has been opened
When the pot is open, each player has three options and declares which one is being chosen:
1 Pass. Passing after the pot is open means dropping out, so the player folds up his or her cards face down in the centre of the table, forming a discard pile, and takes no further part in that deal.
2 Play. In this option the player must put a stake, equal to the opening bet, into the pot.
3 Raise. To raise, the player must stake the same amount as the opening player, plus an additional amount.

Play after the stake has been raised
Each player still has three options:
1 to pass by folding up his or her cards onto the discard pile and dropping out;
2 to play by staking the total of the raised bet. A player who has already placed a bet equal to the opening bet need only add the amount raised; or

3 to re-raise by staking the total of the raised bet plus an additional amount.

Completing the betting

Play continues for as many rounds as necessary, with

Result when the betting is completed

Dad (**C**) was the opener with three chips.
Gran (**D**) raised the stake to five chips.
Jill (**E**) passed and folded.
Uncle Tom (**F**) passed and folded. He remains as dealer and conducts the draw.
Mum (**A**) played, staking five chips.
John (**B**) played, staking five chips.
There are now a total of eighteen chips in the pot.

each player passing, playing or re-raising, until everyone has stopped raising.

If all but one player has dropped out, that player wins and claims the pot.

If the winner was the opener, that player's pair of Js or higher pair must be shown.

If the winner was not the opener, that player does not show any cards.

The draw

When there are two or more players remaining, they participate in the draw.

Players should watch their opponents' decisions and reactions closely during the draw to assess the strength of their hands.

Beginning with the nearest active player to the left and going clockwise in turn, the dealer asks each active player 'how many' that player wants to draw. A player has two options:

1 to stand pat, i.e. keep the five cards. The dealer then passes on to the next player; or

2 to draw up to three cards.

A player choosing to draw must discard, face down, the same number of cards before the dealer draws the new cards from the top of the stock, dealing them face down.

Once cards are discarded they cannot be retaken.

Mistakes

If the dealer shows a draw card by mistake, it is placed face up to one side and is not used in play again until the next deal. The dealer draws a replacement card.

If a player, or the dealer when making his or her own draw, reveals a card, the card still stands.

If a player does not get the correct number of draw cards, the dealer must correct the mistake, unless a card has already been drawn and given to the next player. Players should check they have the correct number immediately.

Four players in the draw

Tom (**F**) asks Mum (**A**) 'how many'?
Mum says 'three' and discards three cards, replacing them with the three draw cards.
John (**B**) will draw one card.
Dad (**C**) and Gran (**D**) both watch everyone's reactions carefully.

The stock pile

If there are nine or ten players and the stock cards run out before everyone has completed the draw, the discards are collected, shuffled, cut and used to complete the draw.

Placing further stakes after the draw

Beginning with the player who opened the pot, and going round clockwise in turn, each player now has six options:

1 Pass. Passing players fold up their cards and drop out of play, leaving their stakes in the pot.

2 Check. Players can check their bets only if nobody has already made a bet.

By saying 'check', the player stays in the game and reserves the right to pass, bet, raise, re-raise or call at the next turn.

3 Bet. If nobody else has already bet, a player can make the first bet after the draw, staking any amount within the agreed limits for the game.

4 Raise. When the first bet has been made, players can then raise the stake as before.

5 Re-raise. When a raise has been staked, a player may re-raise, as before.

6 Call (leading straight to a showdown). A player calls another player to reveal his or her hand by paying into the pot the same stake as the player being called has bet. The challenging player says 'I call you' while paying in the stake.

The player who has been called must reveal his or her hand as it is the first of the showdown.

Four active players after the draw

Dad (**C**) starts, because he was the opener. He passes and folds.
Gran (**D**) checks, remaining an active player.
Mum (**A**) bets and places two chips in the pot.
John (**B**) raises Mum three and places five chips in the pot.

The call
Now there are only three active players: Gran, John and Mum. Gran realizes she can't win, so she passes and folds.
Mum adds three chips to the pot, to make her stake

equal to John's. Then she calls John to show his hand. He has a 9-high straight flush.

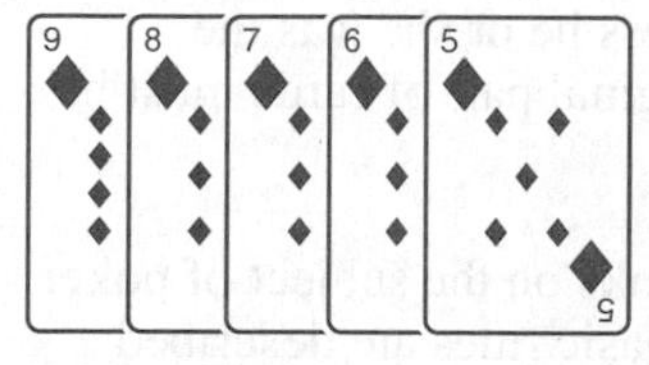

Mum then shows her hand. She wins with a Q-high straight flush.

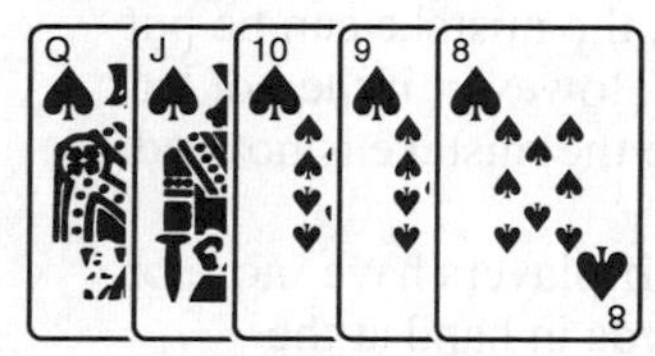

The showdown
Players continue the betting round after the draw until there is a showdown, which occurs in one of three situations, as follows:
1 When all players pass, there is a showdown. The original opener is first to show his or her hand; the rest then follow in clockwise order. The highest ranking hand wins the pot.
2 When one or more players call another player by betting amounts to equal that raised by the latter, the called player declares the rank of his or her hand first, and shows it. The rest then follow in clockwise order. (See the example when Mum calls John.)
The highest ranking hand wins the pot.

3 When a player has made a bet but nobody else bets, raises or calls, that player collects the pot without showing his or her hand, unless he or she was the opener, in which case the original pair of cards must be shown.

Some rules for Draw Poker

There are many advanced books on the subject of poker and its rules. The four most basic rules are described below.

1 Declaring the wrong rank. If a player makes a mistake and declares his or her hand to be of a higher or lower rank than it actually is, the mistake can be put right if noticed immediately. However, if the pot has already been collected before the mistake is noticed, it must stand.

2 Five cards at showdown. If players have more or less than the required five cards in hand at the showdown, their hands are declared dead and they take no part in the showdown. They also lose their stakes.

3 Tapping out. A player who is running out of cash or chips is allowed to play up to the size of the pot until his or her chips run out. This is called a tap-out.

Bets made by any other player after someone has tapped-out are placed to one side.

At the showdown, if the tapped-out player wins, he or she can claim only the original pot and can continue in the game with the won chips.

If the tapped-out player loses at the showdown, he or she has no chips and cannot take part in the game.

4 Discards. Cards that are put on the discard pile, in exchange for cards drawn, must not be seen by anyone. The discard pile may not be inspected.

DRAW POKER VARIATIONS

There are so many variations that only a small selection of those in more regular use are described here.

Unless otherwise specified, all these variations have the same basic rules of Draw Poker.

DEALER'S CHOICE

This version is often played in private homes where a regularly scheduled game takes place.

Each dealer, in turn, has the choice of naming which variation is to be played. People often invent their own slight variations, too.

The dealer describes the variation so that everyone is clear on the rules before the deal.

DEUCES WILD

All or some of the 2s are wild cards; it should be agreed which.

The wild 2s can duplicate any card, including one already held by a player.

With so many wild cards, players may find themselves able to call more than one ranking of hands with the same cards. Players should therefore be careful not to call a lower ranking hand than is possible with their cards because – in this variation – the first-called hand stands.

Sample hands in Deuces Wild

This hand can be called as four 10s.

deuces duplicate as 10s

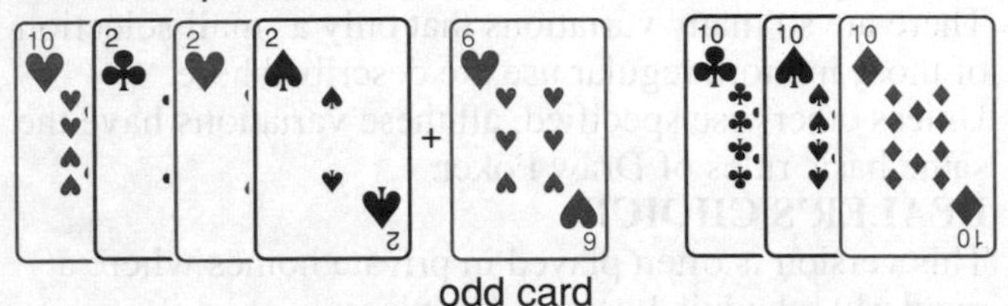

odd card

Or it can be called as a 10-high straight flush.

deuces duplicate as 9, 8 and 7

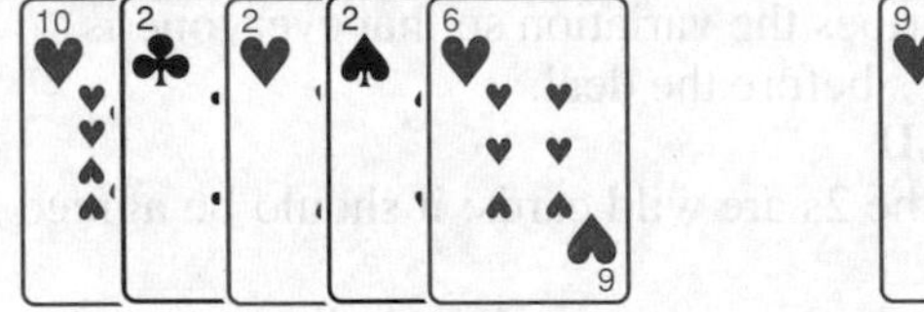

A straight flush is a higher ranking poker hand than a four of a kind.

ENGLISH DRAW POKER

This is played exactly as standard Draw Poker, except at the draw, when the leader is allowed to draw four cards. The maximum draw for all other players is three, as in standard Draw Poker.

JOKER WILD

One or more jokers may be added to the deck in this version. Jokers can stand for any card in the pack. The more jokers there are, the less strategic skill is needed.

BLIND OPENERS

In this version, any player, holding any hand, may open the pot; a pair of Js or better is not needed.

LEADING BLIND OPENER

In this game, the leading player always opens the pot, regardless of what hand is held.

STRAIGHT DRAW POKER

Any player may open the pot with a blind opener in this game, and players may draw up to five cards each at the draw.

POKER WITH A FIVE-CARD DRAW BUY

Players are allowed to draw up to five cards.

SPANISH (OR EUROPEAN) DRAW POKER

This version differs from standard Draw Poker in two ways:

a only two to five people play, four being the best number; and

b the standard 52-card pack is stripped of all cards below the 7s, leaving a deck of 32 cards for play, which includes the aces.

PASS-OUT DRAW POKER

This is sometimes called Bet or Drop. Players may only bet or drop out of the game; they may not check.

PROGRESSIVE DRAW POKER

This is an interesting variation of the conditions required for opening the pot.

If everyone passes on the first deal, then two Qs, or a higher pair, are needed to open the pot on the second deal.

Openers on the second deal

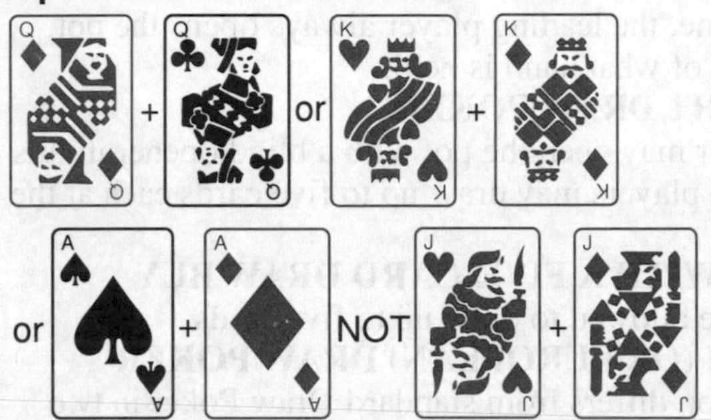

If all players continue to pass at the deals, the pair of cards required to open the pot changes in sequence, as shown here.

Openers on the third deal

Openers on the fourth deal

Openers on the fifth deal

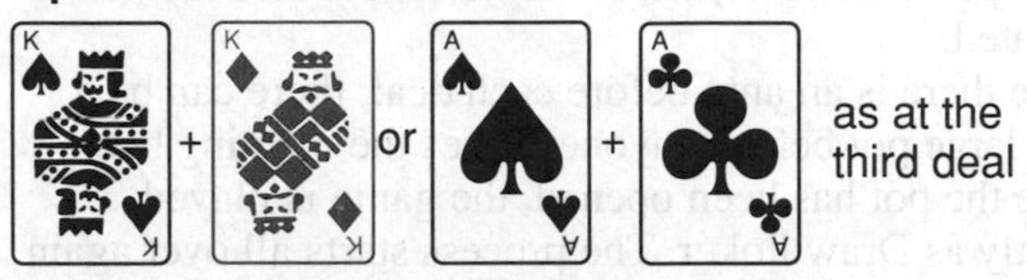

Openers on the sixth deal

as at the second deal

Openers on the seventh deal

If the pot is still unopened, the whole process is repeated.

Since there is an ante before each deal, there can be a very large pot before anyone makes the opening bet. Once the pot has been opened, the game is played exactly as Draw Poker. The process starts all over again in the next deal, i.e. Js or higher are required to open the pot.

FIVES AND TENS

In this variant, also known as Woolworth Draw or St Louis Draw, all 5s and 10s are wild cards.

The player opening the pot must hold one 5 and one 10. Antes and deals continue until someone is dealt the required cards.

High-low Draw Poker variations

All these variations follow the standard Draw Poker rules with the exceptions given.

LOWBALL

This variation is Draw Poker in reverse. The aim is to hold the lowest hand at the showdown.

Cards

Ace is low and counts as 1.

A wild joker is often used, known as the 'bug'.

Openers

Any player can open the pot with any kind of hand.

Rank of hands in Lowball

Flushes and straights do not count. The lowest ranking hand is 5, 4, 3, 2, ace; it is known as a 'bicycle' or 'wheel'.

Each hand shown would win over any hand below it in numerical order (the two hands in 1 are tied). The suit is irrelevant; only the number value of the cards counts. The hand with the joker always ties with the hand it imitates.

Sample Lowball hands in rank order

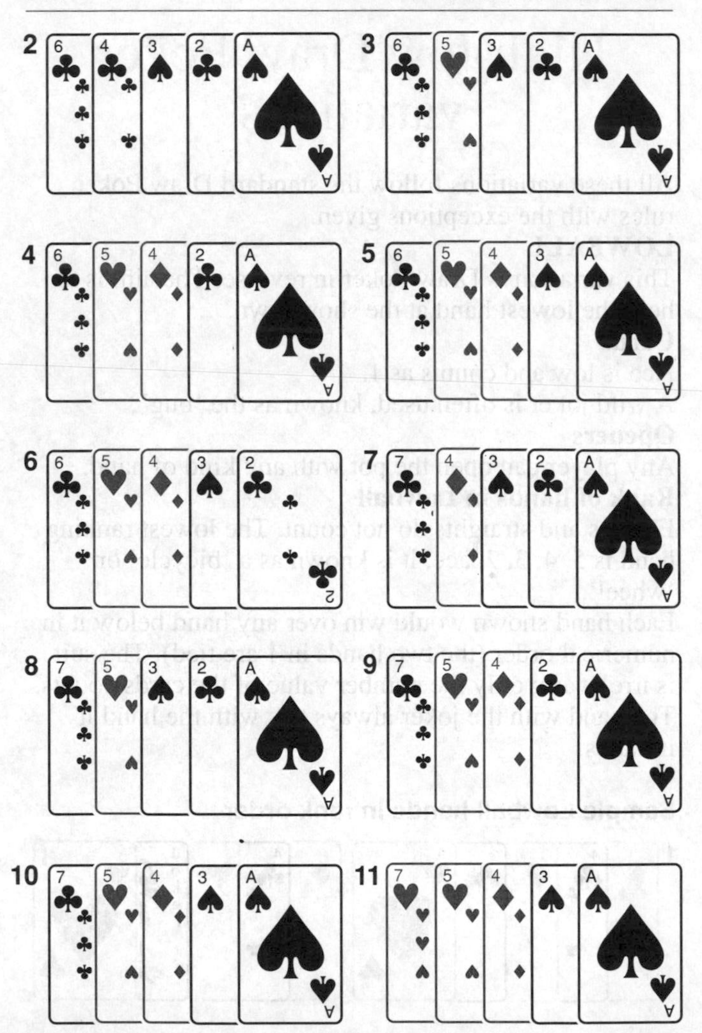
2
3
4
5
6
7
8
9
10
11

DOUBLE-BARREL DRAW

This game is played exactly as Draw Poker. However, if nobody opens the pot and everyone passes on the first round, then the game converts into Lowball Draw Poker on the second round. If all players pass once more, a new deal is dealt and the game reverts to Draw Poker.

HIGH-LOW DRAW POKER

In this variation the winning hands at the showdown are the highest and the lowest hands; the pot is split between them.

Anyone can open the pot with any hand.

The hands are ranked as in standard Draw Poker and the ace can be high or low.

LEG POKER

What is called 'playing for two legs' can be a challenging addition to any poker game, but particularly to Draw Poker and its variations.

The first player to win at the showdown may not take the pot until winning again, i.e. winning a second leg.

The consequences of playing for two legs are:

a several players may win a first leg before someone wins two legs; and

b the pot can increase to a considerable sum.

In High-Low Draw Poker, the competition can be quite fierce, since two players win each game. A player does not have to win two high or two low legs, but can win with one of each.

NINE-HANDED HIGH-LOW DRAW POKER

This variation of High-Low Draw is for seven, eight or nine players.

The game

The deal is the same as in Draw Poker.

The leader must open the pot – with a blind opening or otherwise – but may check after the discard.

The number of raises in this and following rounds is limited to three.

The next round

Each remaining active player in turn either stands pat (by keeping all cards) or discards one or two cards.

Nobody draws any cards to replace the discards.

When everyone has played, the dealer then deals the next two cards from the deck face up into the centre of the table.

Sample situation after the discard round

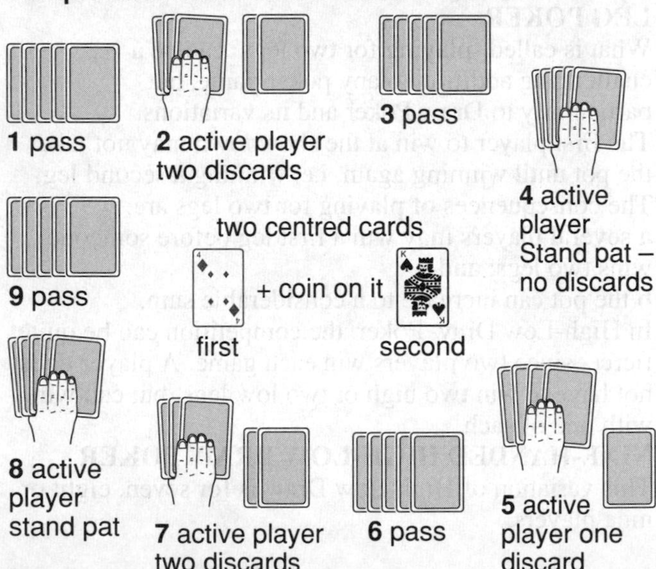

The dealer places a chip on the first card dealt, to identify it. Both centre cards remain on the table during the game.

Players who discard one card 'replace' their discard with the first centre card – i.e., they hold only four cards in hand, but the fifth card is represented by the first centre card. Similarly, players who discard two cards 'replace' their discards with both centre cards – i.e., they hold only three cards in hand, but the other two cards that make up the hand are represented by the two centre cards. Thus, several players may 'hold' the same cards – the centre cards – at one time.

Continuing play

There is another betting round followed by the showdown.

High-low winners

Any hand counts. The players with the lowest and the highest hands are joint winners and share the pot. Straights and flushes can be high or low.

ROCKLEIGH

This is an intriguing High-low variation.

The deal

Each player is dealt only four cards.

The dealer then deals four pairs of cards face down in a row down the centre of the table.

After the first betting round, the dealer turns up any pair, leaving them visible during the second betting round.

This process continues, with the dealer continuing to turn up any pair, until all four pairs are turned up.

Rockleigh betting rounds

first betting round

second betting round

third betting round

fourth betting round

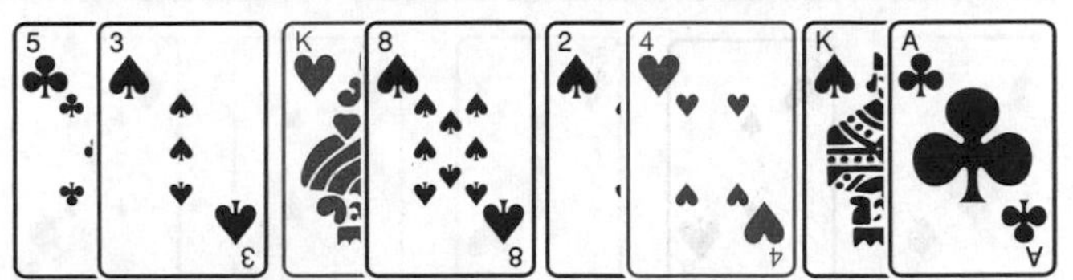

fifth and final betting round

The showdown

Players declare their high or low hand using the best five cards selected from six available, i.e. the four in hand and the two in any one of the upturned pairs. Players wishing to declare both high and low can use one two-card group for high and one for low. A single two-card group may also be used for both high and low.

A sample hand

cards on table

cards in hand

Player rejects Q of diamonds and, without taking the cards from the table, selects the pair: 2 of spades and 4 of hearts.

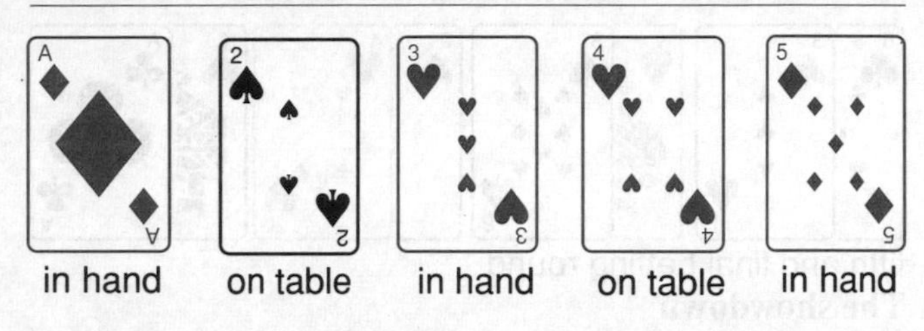

Using ace low, the player declares the hand low.

SPIT IN THE OCEAN

There are dozens of Spit Poker variations that can be played using standard Draw Poker rules or with High-low rules. Spit in the Ocean is the basic spit variation.

Spit rules

Everyone is dealt four cards, then a final card is dealt face up on the table. This is to be the fifth card in every player's hand. It may not be rejected.

Playing

The game proceeds as in standard Draw Poker, except that the player to the left of the dealer must open the pot, regardless of what cards are in hand.

The showdown

Players should hold only four cards. The hand they declare depends on the game being played: Standard, Lowball or High-low Draw Poker.

Stud Poker

This is the fastest and most skilled version of poker. It is also known as Open Poker and is preferred by those who play primarily for money. The pots can be quite large because there are more betting rounds than in Draw Poker.

Draw Poker is more favoured for games among friends and family members. However, learning to play some of the Stud Poker variations can improve a player's strategic skills.

Preparations

All the preliminaries, such as choosing the dealer and sitting positions and agreeing the stake limits and rank of cards, are the same as in Basic Poker.

Stake limits in Stud Poker

Below is a selection of six of the many betting agreements used in Stud.

1 Fixed limits. A minimum and maximum chip or money stake are decided, such as 1 to 2; 1 to 5; 5 to10; 5 to 20; 10 to 25; 50 to 100, etc.

A player may bet the minimum, the maximum or any amount between the two.

There is no ante and no dealer's edge.

2 Choice of two. One of two agreed stakes may be bet, such as 5 and 10; 5 and 25; 50 and 100, etc.

A player may only bet the higher of the two stakes when:

a holding an opening pair or better;

b it is the betting round before the fifth card is dealt;

c it is the final betting round before the showdown.

3 Choice of three. One of three agreed stakes can be bet, such as one of 5, 10 and 20; or one of 10, 20 and 30.
A player must only bid the smallest or the middle stake, up to and including the fourth round of betting, unless holding an opening pair.
The maximum can be staked once the player holds an opening pair or has reached the final round of betting.
4 Dealer's edge. Before the deal, the dealer places into the pot an agreed amount, usually the minimum limit.
5 Player's ante. Before the deal everyone antes the minimum stake into the pot. The amount may be higher by mutual agreement.

Player's ante

6 Pot limit. The quickest way of betting is to begin with a small ante from all players. Then, for each bet, players choose how much to bet up to the maximum already in the pot.

FIVE-CARD STUD POKER

After the ante, if appropriate, each player is dealt one card face down. This is called the 'hole' card and players carefully guard it from the eyes of the others. In Stud Poker, the hole card is the only card not seen by any player other than its owner.

Each player is then dealt one card face up on the table and the remaining deck is placed face down in front of the dealer.

The face-up cards are often called upcards.

First betting round

The player with the highest ranking upcard must open the betting. If two or more players have upcards of the same rank, the player nearest the dealer's left begins. All the other players then bet in clockwise order.

Each player has four options:

1 to drop out, by calling 'out' and placing their two cards face down on the table to begin a discard pile;

2 to play, by calling 'stay' and putting the same stake into the pot as the opener;

3 to raise the pot, for example by two, and calling 'raise two', which means putting in the pot the same amount as the opener plus two more units; or

4 to re-raise the pot, by raising on an already raised bet.

End of first betting round

This happens when either of the following occurs:

a only one player remains active, in which case that player claims the pot and does not have to reveal his or her hole card. In this situation, a completely new deal would take place; or

b the last bet in the pot has been met by all remaining active players. Meeting a bet means betting the same amount as the last bet, whatever it was.

When the round ends with **b**, each player is dealt a third card face up on the table. The dealer does this, and subsequent deals, by taking one card at a time from the top of the deck, using only one hand, without picking up the deck.

Second betting round

The player with the highest ranking pair of upcards starts play. This player has three options:

1 to drop out by calling 'out' and throwing all cards on the discard pile;

2 to check, by calling 'check', which means staying in the game but not betting at the moment. A player cannot check after a bet has been made; or

3 to bet, by placing a bet in the pot.

After someone has opened the betting, each following player must do one of the following:

a stay and meet the bet, by putting an equal bet into the pot;

b drop out, by discarding all cards;

c raise the bet; or

d re-raise the bet.

Any player who may have checked prior to a bet having been made must adhere to rules **a** to **d**.

This betting round proceeds, as before, until:

a all but one player has dropped out;

b there remain two or more active players who have met all bets; or

c nobody has opened the betting but two or more players have checked.

The dealer then deals each person a fourth card, face up, as before.

Third betting round

This is played the same as the second betting round. If two or more active players remain, they are dealt their fifth and final card, face up.

Fourth and last betting round

This is played the same as the previous two rounds, except that the option to play is now the call hand, i.e. players call their hands as they make their bets, starting with the player with the highest ranking four upcards. Players must also call possible flushes and straights. The ranking of the hands is the same as for Basic Poker.

Showdown

Starting from the dealer's left and proceeding clockwise,

each active player in turn must turn over their hole card and declare the rank of their hand. The player with the highest ranking hand wins the pot.

The game then proceeds in the same way until the time limit (agreed upon at the start) is reached. See Basic Poker for details of agreed limits.

STUD POKER VARIATIONS

There are many variations of Stud, and many of the variations have their own variations. People who play together regularly often invent their own supplementary rules. If this is done, they are best written down to prevent arguments later.

Some variations are described here.

FIVE-CARD STUD WITH DEUCES WILD

All the 2s are wild cards. Players must declare at the showdown the value attributed to any wild cards they hold. They cannot change their declaration after their turn has passed.

Sometimes a joker is added as an extra wild card.

FIVE-CARD STUD WITH LAST CARD DOWN

This is played as before but with the last card dealt face down so players have two hole cards.

FIVE-CARD STUD WITH FIVE BETS

In this variation, an extra betting round is inserted after the hole cards have been dealt and before the first upcard is dealt. This means that the first betting round is done on knowledge of one card only.

SKEETS

This version is played exactly as Five-card Stud but after each betting round the dealer has the option of calling 'skeets' and dealing a spit card to the centre of the table.

Any player can include one or more of the spit cards to make the best hand at the showdown.

Sample Stud Poker hands

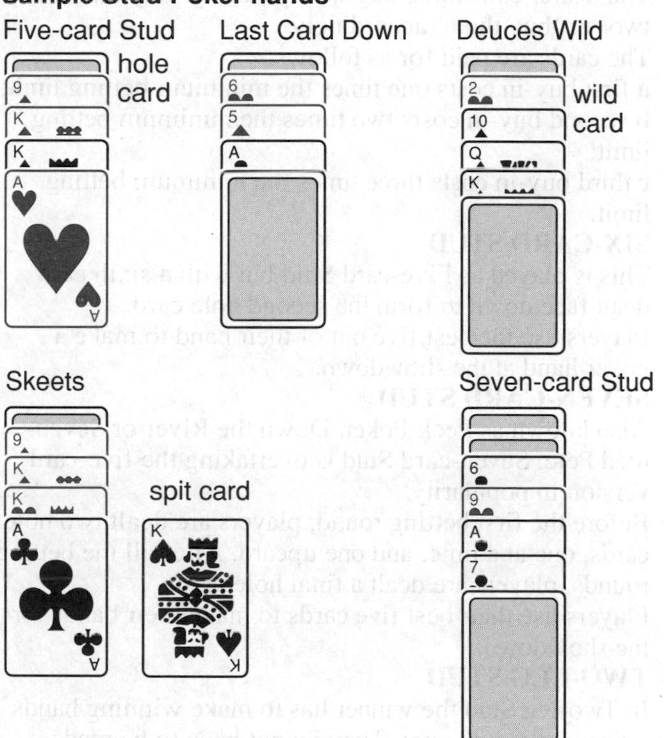

BUY-INS

In this option, after the fifth betting round the dealer calls 'buy one' or 'substitution'.

Each player in turn may buy a card from the dealer by discarding one and then being dealt a new card. If a hole card is substituted, the new card is dealt face down; if an upcard, the new card is dealt face up.

The dealer calls three buy-ins by calling 'buy one', 'buy two' or 'buy three' accordingly.

The cards are paid for as follows:

a first buy-in costs one times the minimum betting limit;
b second buy-in costs two times the minimum betting limit;
c third buy-in costs three times the minimum betting limit.

SIX-CARD STUD

This is played as Five-card Stud but with a sixth card dealt face down to form the second hole card.

Players use the best five out of their hand to make a poker hand at the showdown.

SEVEN-CARD STUD

Also known as Peek Poker, Down the River or Seven-toed Pete, Seven-card Stud is overtaking the five-card version in popularity.

Before the first betting round, players are dealt two hole cards, one at a time, and one upcard. After all the betting rounds, players are dealt a final hole card.

Players use their best five cards to make their hands for the showdown.

TWO-LEG STUD

In Two-leg Stud the winner has to make winning hands twice to claim the pot. They do not have to be made consecutively.

HEINZ

This is a Seven-card Stud game in which all 5s and 7s are wild cards. A player being dealt an upcard that is wild must meet the pot or drop out.

ROLLOVER

Also known as Beat Your Neighbour or No Peekie, this game is similar to Seven-card Stud except that players are dealt seven face-down cards, one at a time, which they do not examine.

Players each shuffle their seven cards in a pile, face down on the table, without looking at them.

The leader begins by rolling over his or her top card face up on the table and bets on it. All players bet in turn as in Stud Poker.

The next player in turn, in clockwise order, then rolls over his or her cards, beginning with the top card in the pile, until a card is revealed that is higher in rank than the card of the previous player.

That player, and the others, again bet in turn.

Players continue, in turn, to roll over their cards and bet.

A player who runs out of cards without rolling over a higher ranking card has to drop out of the game and discard his or her cards.

This process continues until one player remains with an unbeatable hand and claims the pot.

Rollover sample hands with four players

leader

Leader rolls over one card and there is a betting round.

second player

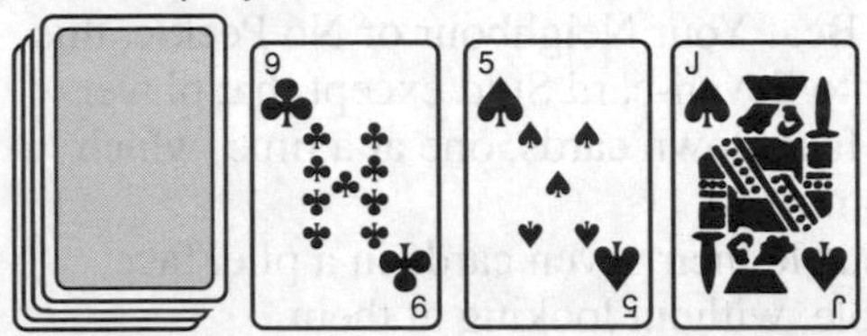

J of spades beats 10 of hearts, so another betting round ensues.

third player

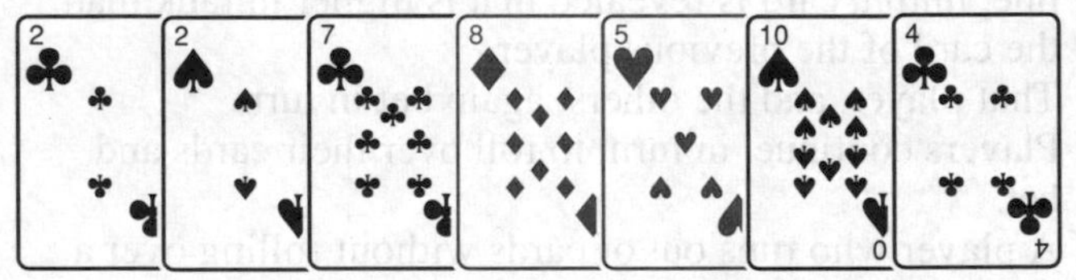

The third player cannot beat the J of spades, so there is not another betting round.

fourth player

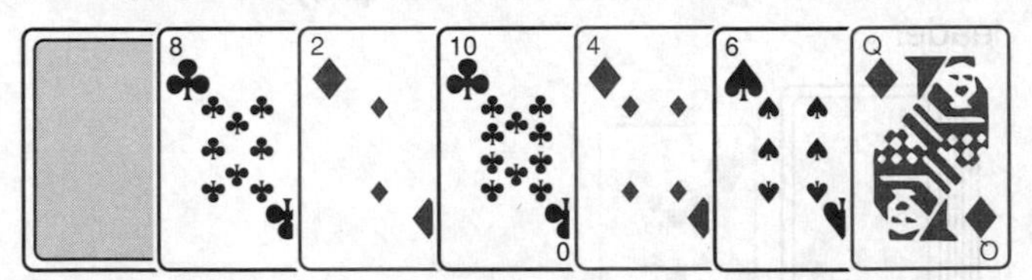

Q of diamonds beats J of spades, so there is another betting round.

first player

K of spades beats Q of diamonds, so there is another betting round.

second player

The second player cannot beat the K of spades, so there is not another betting round.

The third player cannot roll over any more cards, and so is out.

fourth player

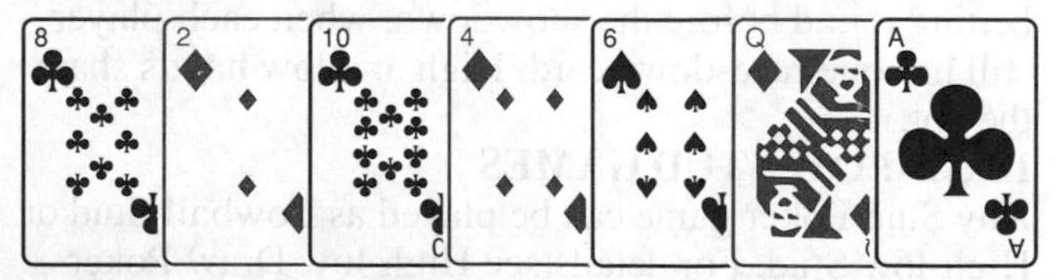

Ace of clubs is unbeatable, so the fourth player wins.

ANACONDA

This is a Seven-card Stud variation.

Each player is dealt seven cards face down, singly.

Players examine their cards and there is a betting round.

Then each player passes any three cards to the player on the left. This is done simultaneously on the command of the dealer.

Another betting round takes place.

Then each player passes two cards to the left, and there is a third betting round.

Each player then passes one card to the left and there is a final betting round before a rollover starts.

(Sometimes the passing of two and then one card is omitted.)

Players then choose their five best cards and put these in any order they like and place them face down on the table.

On a given signal by the dealer, everyone rolls over their top card.

A betting round then takes place, starting with the player with the highest ranking upcard.

Another card is then rolled over by the active players, and another betting round ensues, and so on.

If played as a High-low Stud Game (see below), then players must declare their hands high or low at the last betting round before the showdown, when each player still has one face-down card. High and low hands share the pot.

HIGH-LOW STUD GAMES

Any Stud Poker game can be played as Lowball Stud or High-low Stud. For details see High-low Draw Poker Variations, p. 250.

Other Poker games

LEFTY LOUIE

This is a wild-card variation that can be used with any poker game.
All picture cards whose characters are looking to the left are wild cards.
This gets interesting when two different packs are used during a game, as the way picture cards are printed varies from pack to pack.
Choosing a familiar pack of cards gives a player an advantage over the other players.

Sample of wild cards from one pack

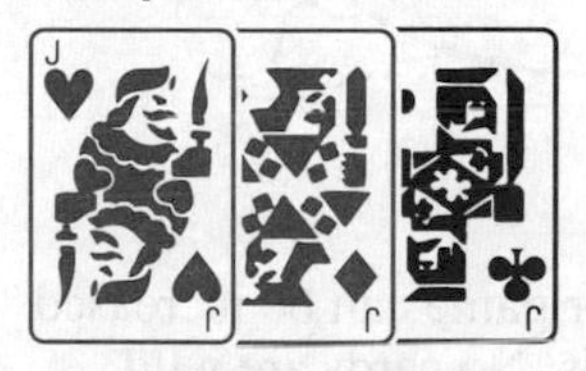

STRIP POKER

This is a fast version of poker in which the stake is not chips but clothing!
What will count as an item of clothing, and the limit to stripping, should be agreed upon before play begins.
The rules are as for Draw Poker but without an ante or any betting.
After the draw, all the players turn their cards face up on the table. The person with the lowest ranking hand is required to take off a piece of clothing (see overleaf).

Strip Poker in progress

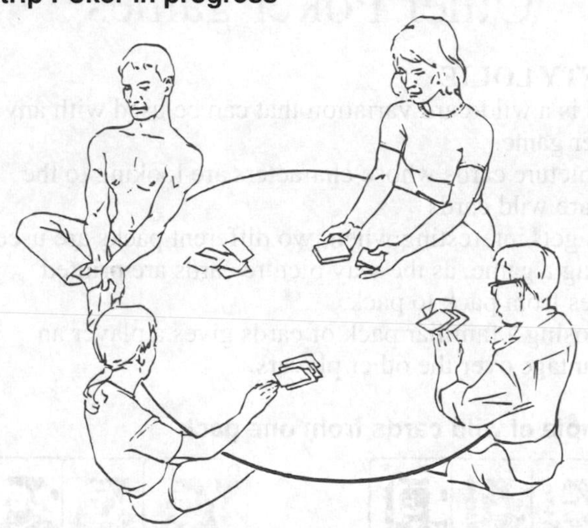

USING A STRIPPED DECK

The speed and skill of any poker game can be increased by using a stripped deck of cards. No cards are wild.

The 40-card deck

In this deck, all the 2s, 3s and 4s are stripped and the ace ranks high.

The 32-card deck

This deck is made by removing all the 2s, 3s, 4s, 5s and 6s. Ace ranks high. This deck makes for a very fast game. High stakes are frequently placed.

The 'Italian' deck

This is a 40-card deck made by stripping all the 8s, 9s and 10s. Ace can rank high or low.

The Italian deck

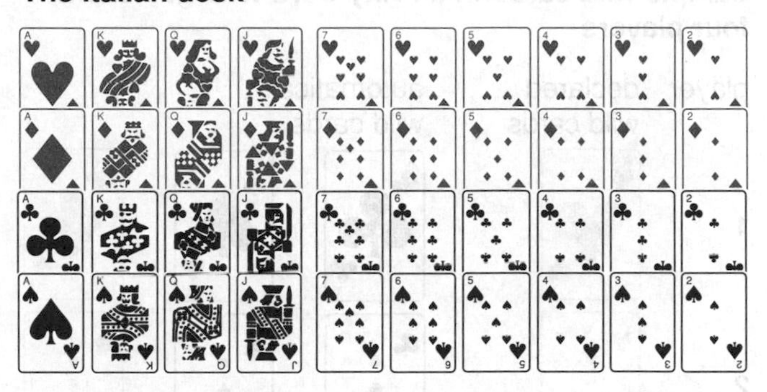

WILD WILD POKER

The wildest and most hectic games of poker are those in which wild cards are chosen by the players during the game.

Players new to Wild Wild Poker should keep the stakes low until they become familiar with the effects these wild cards have on their chosen variation of poker.

ANY CARD WILD

This is the wide-open version in which each player can make any one of the cards in hand into a wild card, declaring which is the wild card at the showdown.

In another version, players declare immediately after the deal which card in their hands they are making into a wild card.

The rank of these cards is written down, because all other cards of the same rank automatically become wild cards.

In this version of Any Card Wild, one of every player's cards is known.

Sample wild cards in an Any Card Wild game with four players

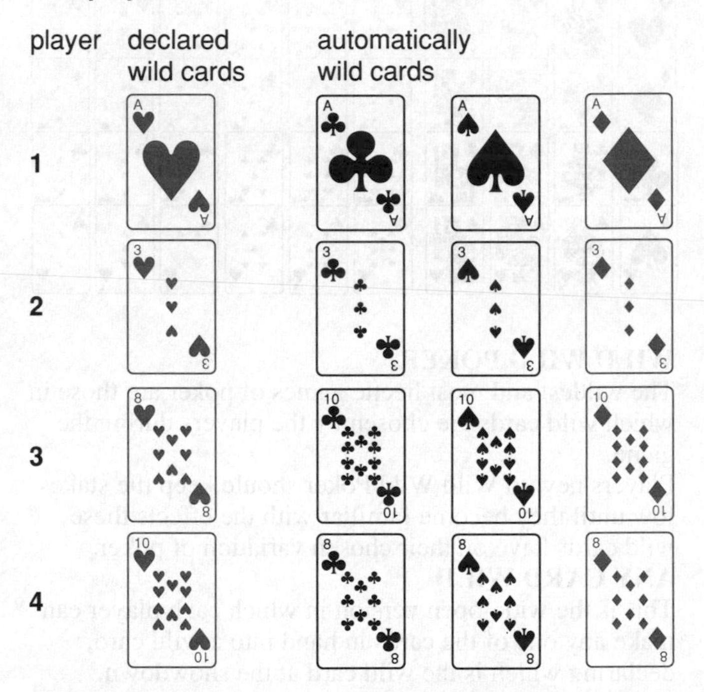

If there are four players, there would be 16 wild cards; if there are seven players, the number of wilds jumps to 28.

ANY SUIT WILD

In this version, known also as Hectic Poker, any suit is wild, making 13 cards into wild cards. Either all players agree before the deal which suit is to be wild for the hand, or each player can declare his or her own wild suit at the showdown.

Red Dog

Also known as High-card Pool, Red Dog was the favoured gambling game of reporters and their associates in the pre-television days when newspapers were the main source of news.

It is a game of skill for up to ten players.

Cards

A standard deck of 52 cards is used. Ace ranks high.

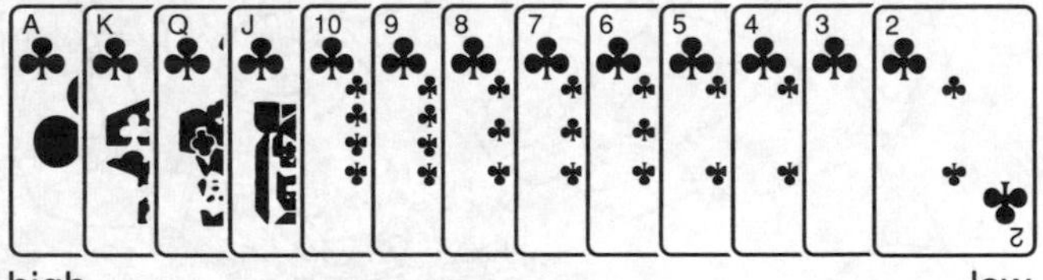

Competition

Players compete to win the contents of the pot.

Everyone antes the pot and adds a stake when it is their turn, so the total staked is often high.

Large amounts can be won and lost quickly in Red Dog.

Friends getting together to play socially should decide whether to play with:

1 chips with no monetary value;

2 low-value coins; or

3 chips purchased from a common pool.

The excitement of Red Dog comes from the build-up of the pot when each player loses a bet, so large numbers of chips should be in circulation.

Aim

Players try to win the pot by gambling on their chances of holding a card that is higher ranking than – but of the same suit as – the one turned up from the stock.

The ante

Before the deal, everyone antes the pot by the same amount. The ante can be as low as one chip each or as high as is agreeable to all players.

Dealing

Everyone cuts the pack. The player cutting the highest ranking card is the dealer.

Starting with the player on the dealer's left, five cards

A sample hand

Player bets that the hand holds a higher card than the stock card, and in the same suit.

Some sample stock cards

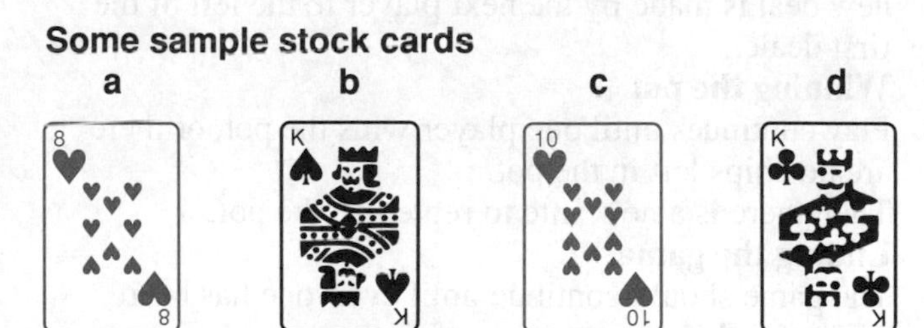

If the stock card is **a** or **d** this player would win.
If the stock card is **b** or **c** this player would lose.

are dealt to each player, when there are up to eight players.
The deal is four cards each for nine or ten players.

Playing

The dealer places the remaining cards face down and only the dealer turns cards up from this stock.
Players study their cards and, in turn, starting from the dealer's left, bet that they hold a higher ranking card of the same suit as the card at the top of the stock.
The first player bets by placing chips on the table. Any number of chips can be staked, from one to the total already in the pot.
The dealer turns up the top card of the stock and places it face up on the table.
If the player wins, the winning card is shown and the player claims his or her own bet plus the same number of chips from the pot.
If the player loses, his or her entire hand is shown and thrown in, and the chips bet are added to the pot.
When everyone has had a turn, including the dealer, a new deal is made by the next player to the left of the first dealer.

Winning the pot

Play continues until one player wins the pot, or there are no chips left in the pot.
Then there is a new ante to replenish the pot.

Ending the game

The game should continue until everyone has been dealer for the same number of times.

Strategy

Every card played is visible, so players who have a good memory for cards have the edge on those who

haven't. Later players, especially the dealer, have great advantage over leading players because they see all the cards that have been played.

Remembering what has been played helps players to decide if their hands have a good chance of winning. For example, if holding five court cards, the dealer's chances of winning increase if aces are turned up for earlier players.

A strong hand

Mistakes

If the top card of the stock is exposed by mistake, it is put aside and the next card is turned up.

Once a bet has been made, it cannot be changed. Any bet paid to the pool by mistake must stand. Any bet paid out by mistake must stand if the next top card has been exposed.

Fair play

Cheating is easy if three cheats work together, sending each other signals about which cards they hold. For this reason, players should be warned against joining games with strangers.

VARIATIONS

HIGH OR LOW RED DOG

Players may bet that they hold either a higher or a lower card than the stock card. In either case their card must be of the same suit as the stock card.

GI RED DOG

During World War II a version called GI Red Dog developed, which gave the dealer even better chances than in standard Red Dog.

Everyone is dealt only three cards and the dealer has three turns before the deal passes to the next player.

To compensate for this advantage, only the dealer antes, putting any stake into the pot.

Play then proceeds as in traditional Red Dog.

Some players of GI Red Dog say the dealer should have four cards, giving even more of an advantage.

BURN CARD RED DOG

In this variation, at each player's turn the dealer discards the top card of the stock – 'burns' it – after showing it to all players. The dealer then turns up the next top card, which determines whether the player has won or lost.

Slobberhannes

Slobberhannes is popular in Holland and Germany. It is for three to six players. Paper and pencil are needed for scoring.

Cards

All cards below the 7s are stripped from a standard pack of 52, leaving a deck of 32 cards ranking from ace down to 7.

When there are three, five or six players, both black 7s are also stripped from the deck so that everyone is dealt the same number of cards.

Rank

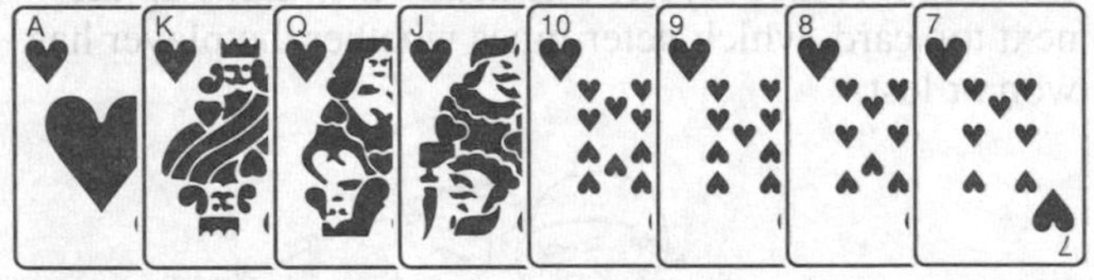

Competition

There is no betting in this game. All players might lose points during play, but the one who loses the most pays the others in coins or chips.

Aim

Players make tricks but try not to take the first or last one, nor a trick containing the Q of clubs: these tricks all give a penalty point.

Tricks

A trick is one card from each player in turn.

Some sample tricks

three players

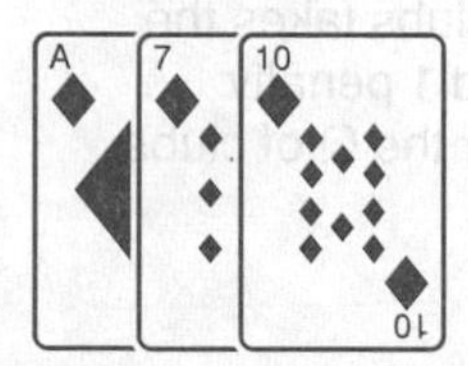

ace of diamonds takes the trick

Q of clubs takes the trick and 1 penalty point

four players

ace of spades takes the trick

J of hearts takes the trick

five players

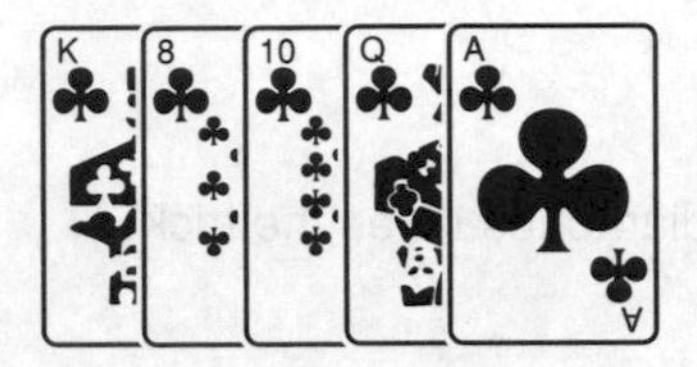

ace of clubs takes the trick and 1 penalty point for the Q of clubs

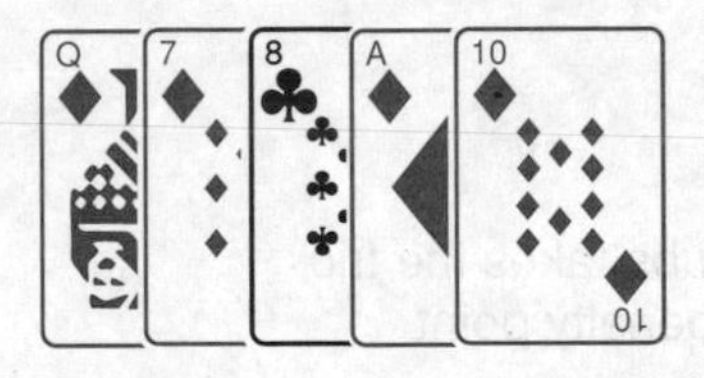

ace of diamonds takes the trick

six players

K of spades takes the trick

10 of hearts takes the trick

Dealing
The dealer, chosen by cut, deals all the cards starting with the player to the left.

Playing
Players examine their cards and the player to the dealer's left leads by playing any card from the hand to start the first trick.

The next player must play a card of the same suit if possible. If not, any other card may be discarded.

The highest ranking card of the leading suit takes the trick and that player leads to the next trick. There are no trumps in Slobberhannes. Skill is required to discard effectively and to play the Q of clubs without winning the trick.

Ending a hand
The hand ends when all tricks have been made. The deal passes clockwise to the next player, who deals all the cards again, starting with the player on the left.

Players keep track of their scores for each hand.

Scoring
Players who take the first or the last trick of a hand, or a trick containing the Q of clubs, lose 1 point for each of these tricks.

If a player takes all three of these tricks in the deal, it is called Slobberhannes. Anyone getting Slobberhannes loses an extra point.

Losing the game
The first player to lose 10 points loses the game and pays all the other players the difference between his or her score and theirs.

Vingt-et-un

Also known as Pontoon, this is a game of chance for any number of players. A version of it is played as the banking game called 21 or Blackjack.

Cards

A standard deck of 52 cards is needed. If there are more than seven players, two decks can be used.

The cards have points values as follows: aces count as 11 or 1; court cards count as 10; all others count at face value.

Individual players may choose to use an ace to count as 11 points or 1 point.

A pontoon

A pontoon consists of two cards that add up to 21. Any ace with any court card or a 10 makes a pontoon.

Pontoons

The bank

The dealer is chosen by cutting the cards; the player cutting the highest card deals.

The dealer is also the banker and everyone plays against the bank.

Everyone then agrees what the maximum stake shall

be. Five chips or small coins, for example, would be a good starting maximum.

Dealing

The banker shuffles the pack and gives each player – including him- or herself – one card face down, starting with the player on the left.

The aim is to collect cards that total 21 points or approach that, but to avoid going over 21.

Playing

Each player looks at his or her own card, replaces it face down and places a stake by it in turn. The stake can be any amount up to the agreed maximum.

Players stake their money (or chips) on getting cards that total 21.

The banker, however, does not place a stake. If the banker has a good card, he or she makes a bet by calling 'double you'.

This means everyone must double the stake already placed by their cards.

A second card is then dealt face down to each player, and they inspect both cards.

If anyone, including the banker, has a pontoon – i.e. an ace and a 10 or a court card – it is revealed and declared.

Payout on a pontoon

1 If it is the banker who has the pontoon, all players pay twice what each has already staked (or four times, if the banker has doubled).

2 If both the banker and another player have a pontoon, that player only 'pays once', i.e. pays the bank the original stake (or twice that stake if the bank has doubled). All other players 'pay twice'.

3 If a player, but not the banker, has a pontoon, the banker pays that player twice the stake (or four times, if the bank has doubled).
4 If two players have pontoons, and the banker has none, the banker pays them both.

Continuing play

If a pontoon has not been made, the hand continues. Before proceeding, however, some players may want to make splits.

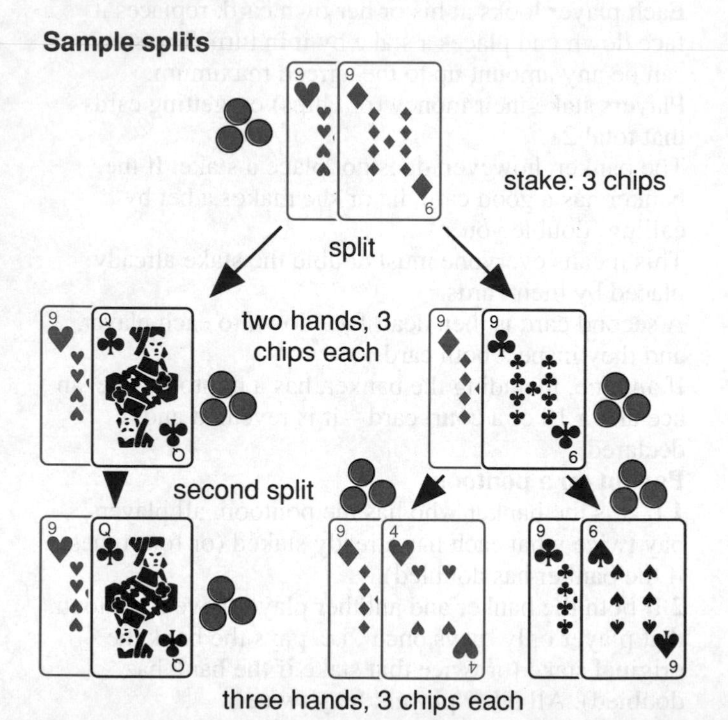

Splits

Anyone who holds two cards of the same rank, such as two 9s or two Js, may split them and have a card dealt on each of them.

If one of the dealt cards is another 9, there could be a further split.

A split must be declared. It is then played as two (or three) separate hands, each carrying the original stake (doubled if the bank has doubled).

Two or more players who want to split in the same round can do so in turn.

If a pontoon is made it must be declared as before.

Play continued: stick, twist or buy

Players now have the option of how their next card is dealt.

The banker begins with the player to the left and asks if players want to 'stick', 'twist' or 'buy'.

If a player's cards add up to 21 or almost 21, the player calls 'stick' (to take no further cards), and the next player takes a turn. Players can only declare 'stick' if the points count of their cards is 16 or more. If the count is 15 or less, players must twist or buy.

'Twist' means a card dealt face up.

'Buy' means a card dealt face down but the player must increase the stake. The amount must not be more than double what is already staked.

If a player buys for an extra stake of, say, two chips, no more than two chips can be staked for any further buys.

A player who has twisted is not allowed to buy on that hand, but may twist on two further turns only.

A player who has bought has the choice of twist or buy again, under the same conditions as before.

Some hands

20 points: stick

25 points: burst

24 points: burst

17 points: stick

19 points: stick

20 points: stick

18 points: stick

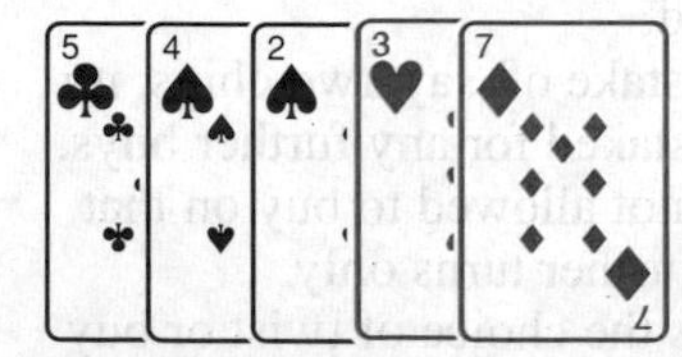

21 points: stick

Five-card, non-bursting hands pay double stakes.

The aim is to acquire cards that add up to but do not exceed 21.

Burst

If a player is dealt a card that takes the total for the hand above 21, the player calls 'burst', throws the cards face up on the table and pays the stake to the bank, taking no further part.

The payout

When everyone has had a turn, the banker puts his or her cards face up on the table and buys or twists cards until either sticking or bursting.

If the banker bursts, each remaining player is paid an amount equal to the player's stake.

If the banker sticks, the remaining players compare the points value of their cards with the banker's. The banker then pays the amount of their stakes to those whose hand has a higher points value than the bank's. Players whose points value is equal to or less than the bank's pay their stakes to the banker.

The five-card trick

The maximum cards a player may collect is five.

Any player who collects five cards without bursting is paid double the stake by the bank, regardless of the points value of the cards.

Limitation on buying

A player may buy three cards to make up a five-card trick. However, if the fourth card gives the player a points total of 11 or less, the player is obliged to twist for the fifth card, because it is certain to make 21 or less. A player is not allowed to bet on a certainty.

Changing the bank

A player who gets a pontoon usually takes over the

bank after the deal has been completed, and then shuffles the cards and makes a new deal. There are three conditions under which the deal remains with the same banker:

a when a pontoon is declared in the first round of a new bank;

b when there are two or more pontoons in the same round; or

c when a pontoon has been built on only one of a pair of split cards.

The joker variation

Some players like to include the joker in the pack, which is wild, i.e. it can stand for any card the player chooses.

Beleaguered Castle

Also known as Laying Siege or Sham Battle.

Cards

A standard 52-card deck is needed.

A sample layout

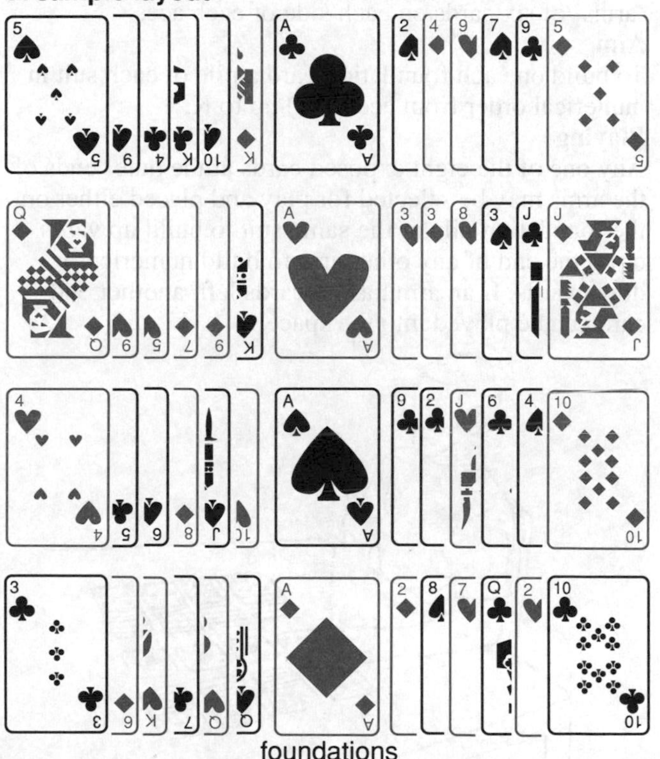

The layout

The four aces, known as the foundation cards, are placed face up in any order in a column. On the left of each ace, deal one card, face up. Then deal the same way to the right of each ace. Deal one card overlapping each of these, and continue dealing in this way, overlapping the cards as they are dealt, until there are 'arms' of six cards on each side of each ace.

Aim

To build on each foundation card a pile of each suit in numerical order from ace (low) up to K.

Playing

Any one of the eight exposed cards at the outer ends of the arms may be selected for play and placed either on the foundation pile of the same suit to build upwards, or on the end of any other arm to build numerically downwards. If an arm has no cards left, another end card can be played into the space.

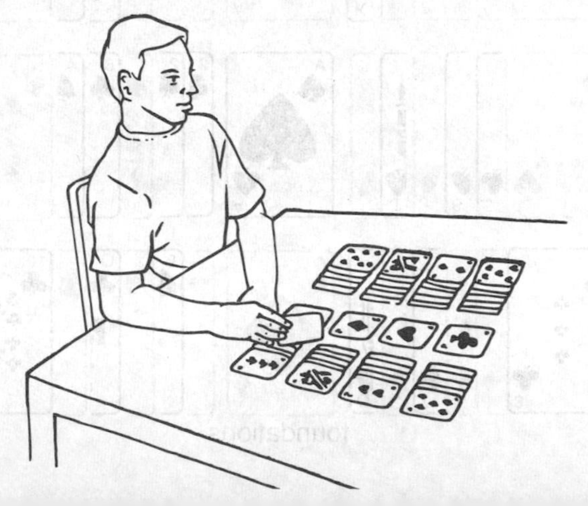

Bisley

Another game using foundation cards.

Cards

One standard deck of 52 cards is used.

The layout

First place the four aces in a row on the table, then increase the length of the row by nine cards dealt from the pack. Continue to deal the cards, making three more rows below the first one, until you have four rows, each of 13 cards. A sample layout is shown overleaf.

Aim

To build suits in rank order, using the aces and the Ks as foundation cards.

Playing

Any of the bottom row of cards can be used to build on an ace of the same suit, numerically upwards, or to build onto another bottom-row card of the same suit, either upwards or downwards (the order of building may be reversed when desired or required).

When a K becomes available, it is placed in a new row above the ace of the same suit and can then be built on numerically downwards. When the two sequences of one suit meet, they can be put into one pile. Spaces at the bottom of columns are not filled, thereby making the cards above them available for play.

A sample layout for Bisley

foundations

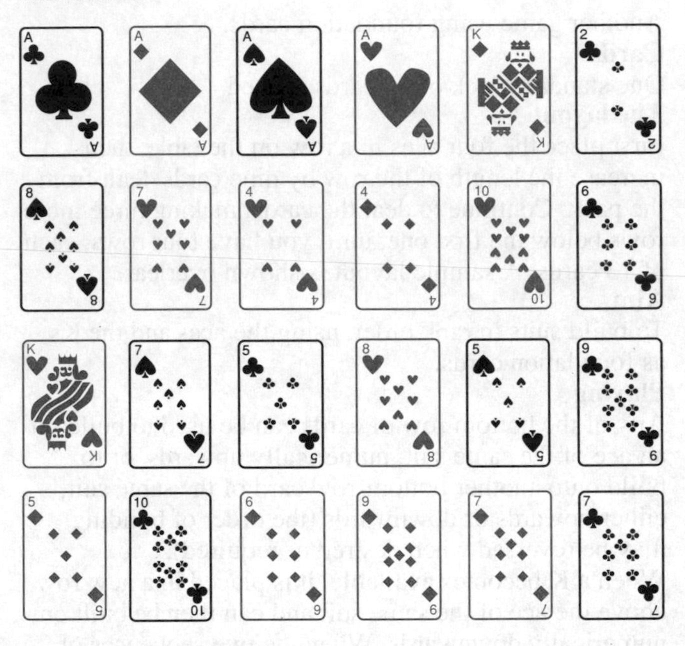

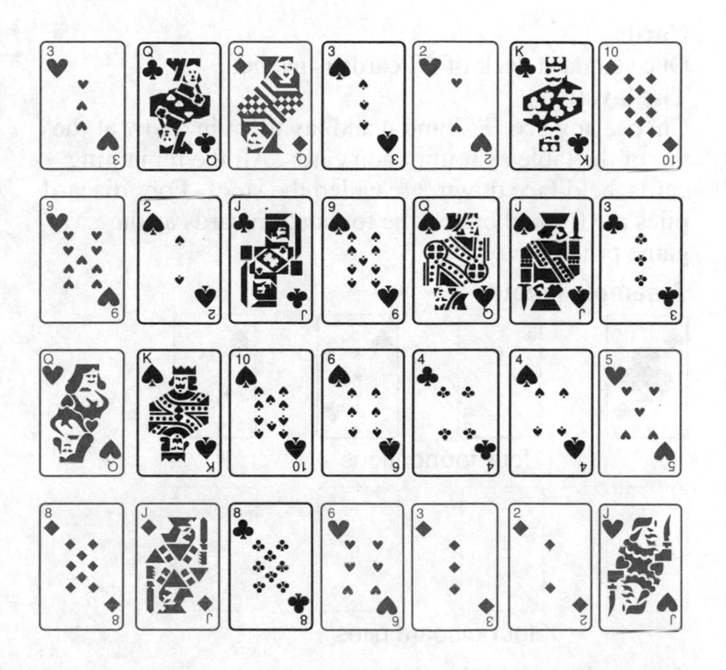

Calculation

Cards

One standard deck of 52 cards is needed.

The layout

Choose any ace, 2, 3 and 4 and lay them in a row at the top of the table as foundation cards. All the remaining cards, held face down, are called the stock. Four discard piles are formed below the foundation cards as the game progresses.

A sample layout

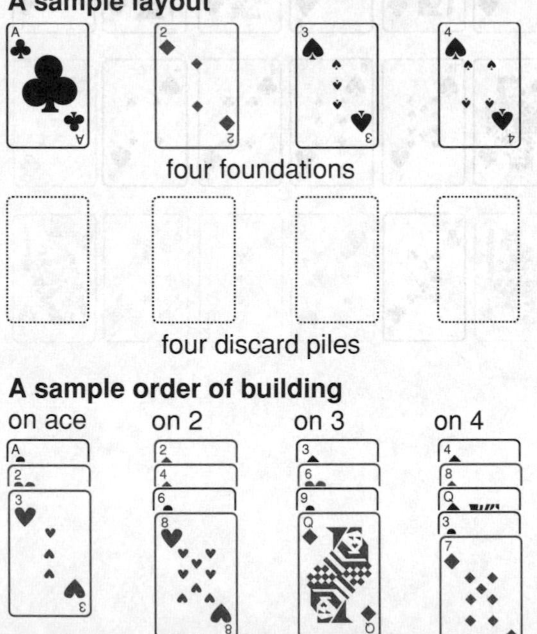

Aim

Disregarding suit, the aim is to build on each foundation card in the following order:

On ACE, every card: ace, 2, 3, 4, 5, 6, 7, 8, 9, 10, J, Q, K.

On 2, every second card: 2, 4, 6, 8, 10, Q, ace, 3, 5, 7, 9, J, K.

On 3, every third card: 3, 6, 9, Q, 2, 5, 8, J, ace, 4, 7, 10, K.

On 4, every fourth card: 4, 8, Q, 3, 7, J, 2, 6, 10, ace, 5, 9, K.

Playing

One card at a time is turned up from the stock and may be placed overlapping any of the foundation cards, to begin building. If a card cannot be used to build, it may be placed face up on any of the four discard piles.

The top card of any discard pile may also be used to build, but may not be transferred to another discard pile.

The skill lies in controlling the cards in the discard piles. For example, Ks will be required last so it will be helpful to keep them either all in one pile or at the bottom of each pile.

Ideally, cards should be built on the discard piles in the order they will be needed to build on the foundations, i.e. in the reverse of the order shown above. Also, it is advisable to scatter cards of the same rank throughout the different discard piles.

In practice, many of the cards turned up from the stock will enable the player to build on the foundation cards.

If a discard pile runs out, the space can be filled with a new pile, if required. The maximum number of discard piles at any one time is four.

Canfield

Named in the USA after a 19th-century gambler and art collector, this game is often known in the UK as Demon.

Cards

One standard deck of 52 cards is used.

A sample layout

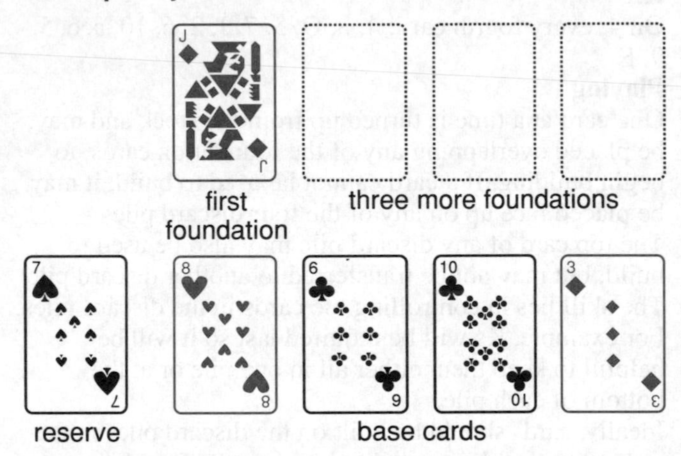

The layout

First a pile of 13 cards (the reserve) is dealt face down, then turned over leaving one card exposed.

The next four cards are placed face up in a row next to the reserve; these form the base cards.

The next card is placed above the first base card and forms the first of a row of four foundations. Its rank determines the rank of all the foundation cards. If a base card already dealt matches the foundation card, it is moved up into the foundation row, and another is dealt in its place. The remaining cards form the stock.

Aim

To build upwards, in suits, on the foundation cards, and to build downwards on the base cards, disregarding suit but in alternate colours, until all the cards are used from the stock, the reserve and the discard pile (if there is one).

Playing

Three cards at a time are dealt from the stock, with only the top card exposed and available to be played. It may be played onto a foundation pile, a base pile or the discard pile. If it is the same rank as the first foundation card, it forms the next foundation.

Building on the foundations is done numerically upwards, in suits, K followed by ace, 2, etc.

Building on the base cards is done numerically downwards, in alternate colours of either suit. A sequence on a base card can be transferred to another basc sequence, providing the colours still alternate and the sequence continues.

Cards from the reserve are used to fill spaces in the base. When the reserve is exhausted, the top card from the discard pile may be used to make a new base if required, or the base may be left empty.

When fewer than three cards remain in the stock, they are dealt one at a time.

How the cards might be played in Canfield

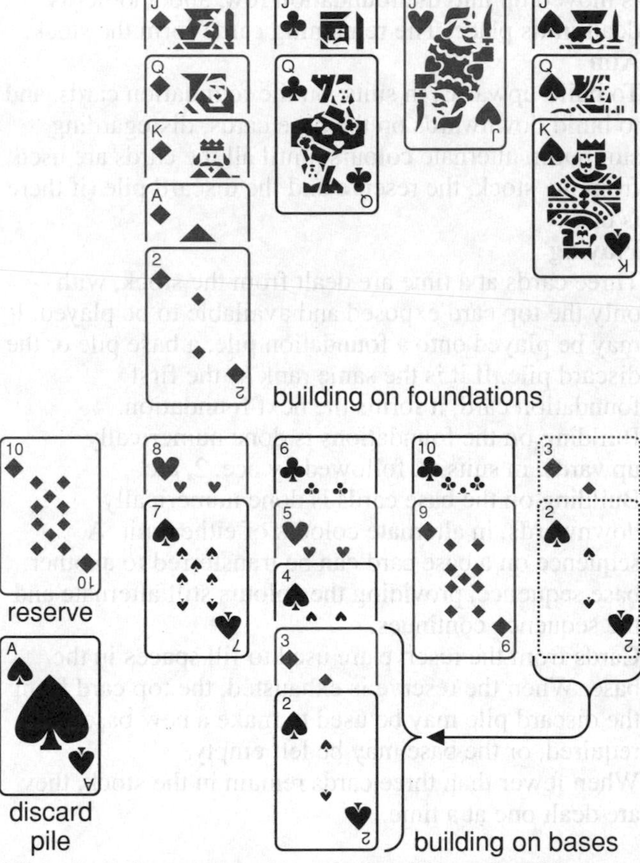

The whole layout may be redealt without shuffling, as often as desired, until the game either comes out or becomes blocked.

Clock

This game has many names, such as Sundial, Travellers, Four of a Kind and Hidden Cards. It is a fast-moving, enjoyable game, but the chances of getting all the cards out are small.

Cards

A standard deck of 52 cards is used.

The layout

The cards are dealt face down, 12 piles of four making a clock face and the 13th pile of four cards in the centre. The cards may be dealt singly, dealing round the circle four times, or in groups of four at a time.

Aim

To reorganize the cards so each pile is of the same rank and matches the position of the hours of the clock: aces at 1 o'clock, 2s at 2 o'clock and so on to Qs at 12 o'clock, leaving the Ks in the central pile.

Playing

The top card of the central pile is turned up and placed under its appropriate position, for example an 8 would be placed under the 8 o'clock pile. The top card from that pile is then turned up and correctly placed, and so on.

If a card is turned up that belongs to the same pile, the procedure is the same.

The game can only be resolved if the last card to be turned up is the fourth K. If the fourth K is turned up before all the other piles are complete, the game would be blocked. Therefore, when a K is turned up, an exchange is allowed. The K may be exchanged for any

The layout for Clock

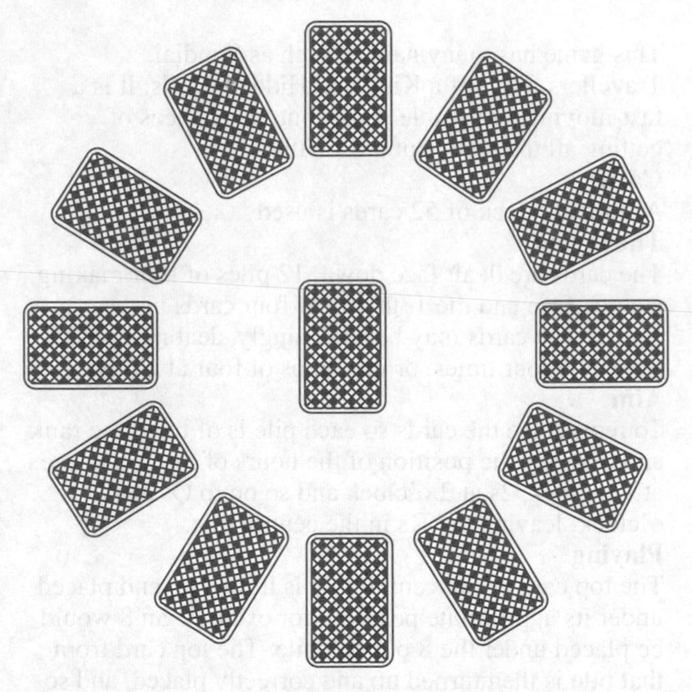

one face-down card on the table. This gives the player a slightly improved chance of winning the game, but the odds against the last card being the fourth K are still very high.
Consequently, players often repeat the game many times at great speed, hoping to win at least once!

Flower Garden

The layout for this game is called the flower garden, individual fans of cards being the "flower beds" and stock cards the "bouquet".

Cards

One standard deck of 52 cards is used.

The layout

Six fans of six cards each are dealt to form the flower beds. The bouquet is the remaining stock, which may be held in the hand or spread face up on the table. It can be sorted into suits.

Aim

To free the four aces and use them as foundations to build upwards in suits, ace up to K.

Playing

In the sample layout, the two aces in the bouquet would immediately be placed face up below the fans, starting two of the foundations.

Any card from the bouquet or any exposed card from the ends of the flower beds can be played. A card may be used to build numerically upwards in suits on a foundation ace, or to build downwards on the exposed card of any flower bed, disregarding suit.

As long as the numerical order remains correct, a sequence of cards may be moved from one flower bed to another.

When a bed is used up, its space may be filled by one card from the bouquet or a bed, or by a sequence from another bed.

A sample layout for Flower Garden

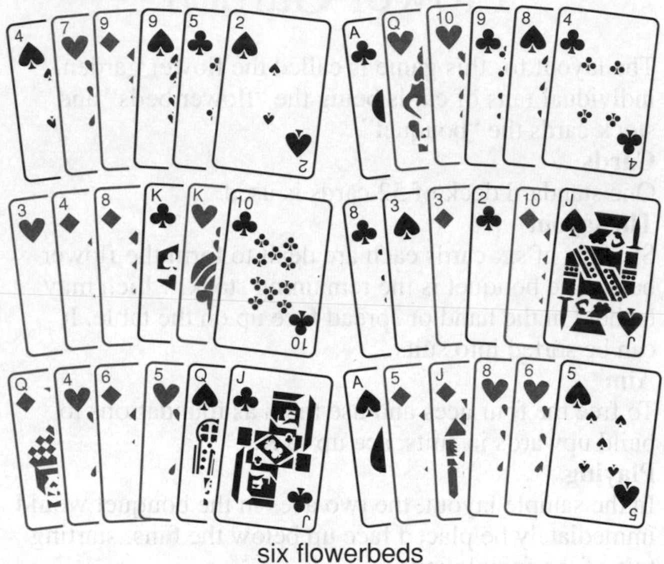

six flowerbeds

foundations

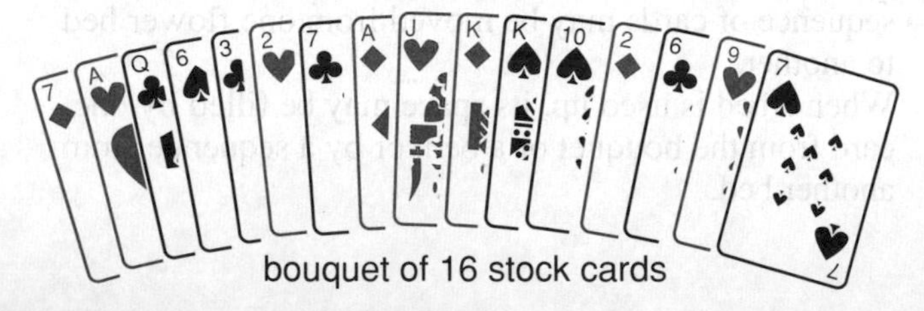

bouquet of 16 stock cards

Fours

A fast game using a piquet deck of 32 cards.

Cards

Remove all the 6s, 5s, 4s, 3s and 2s from a standard deck. Shuffle the remaining 32 cards.

The layout

Deal four cards face up in a row. The stock should be kept face down in the hand or on the table.

Sample layout of a game of Fours in progress

Aim

To make the cards come out in packets of four cards of the same rank.

Playing

If two cards in the layout are of the same rank, place them on top of each other, leaving a space in the row. Turn up four cards from the stock, placing them in order in a row of four on top of (but not completely covering) the first cards and the space.

If any of these four cards in the new row are of equal rank, they are piled together on one of the columns and the spaces filled as the next row of four cards is turned up from the stock. The piles are not removed from the columns and row until there are four cards of equal rank, forming a "packet". In the sample game shown above, it is possible to create a packet of 9s by freeing them through moving and piling the cards that are on top of them, before the next row is dealt. Once a packet has been created, it is put aside and the next row is dealt, which will fill the space left by the packet.

Packets

These are collected in a pile, face up on top of each other. When the stock runs out, the pile of packets is turned face down and used as the stock, without shuffling. Play continues until all the packets have been made or the game is blocked.

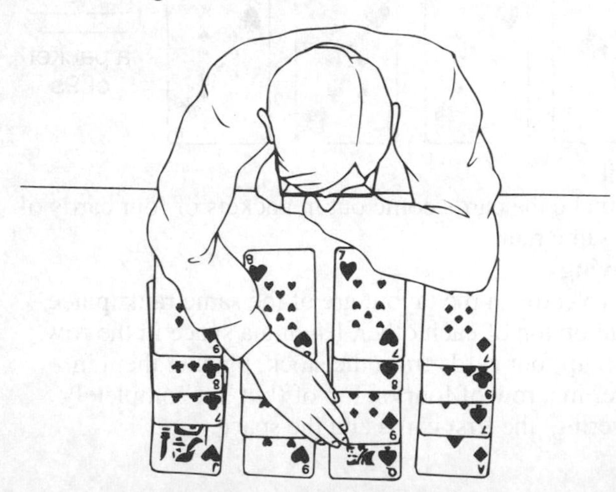

Golf

A great game for housebound golfers.

Cards

A standard deck of 52 cards is used.

The layout

Turn seven cards face up, placing them in a row to become the start of seven columns. Build the columns by placing another card face up below each one. Repeat until there are five cards in each of the seven columns, all clearly visible. This arrangement is called the links. The remaining 17 cards are placed face down in a pile and form the stock of golf clubs.

Aim

To get the lowest possible score by using the stock of golf clubs to "clear" the links. For a nine-hole round, the game would be played nine times.

Playing

Turn one card face up from the stock to form the hole. Any card from the links can then be played onto this card, regardless of suit, providing it follows in numerical sequence, upwards or downwards. Ace counts as low, so the top card of a sequence would be a K.

The direction can be reversed – for example, cards from the links might be available to build on a 3 in a downwards sequence, 2, ace, followed by an upwards sequence, 2, 3, 4, 5.

When it becomes impossible to play any more cards from the links, another card is turned up from the stock, placed on the hole and the process of building in sequence begins again.

When there is a choice about which way to build the sequence, it is helpful to remember which cards have already been played.

When the stock is exhausted, the number value of the cards remaining on the links is totalled. J, Q, K count as 10 each. The total is the score for the hole. If the links have been cleared and no cards remain in the stock, the score is 0. As in golf, the lower the score the better.

For a nine-hole game, the cards are shuffled and a new layout is dealt eight more times.

A sample layout for Golf

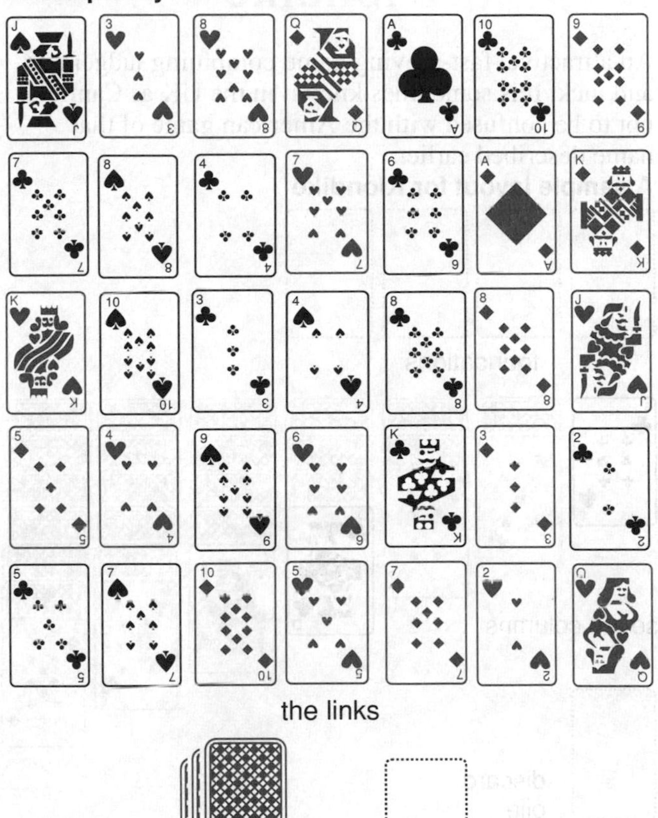

the links

the stock of golf clubs

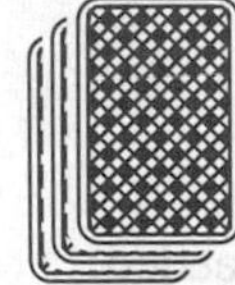

the hole

Klondike

An attractive, fast-moving game combining judgement and luck. It is sometimes known in the UK as Canfield, not to be confused with the American game of that name described earlier.

A sample layout for Klondike

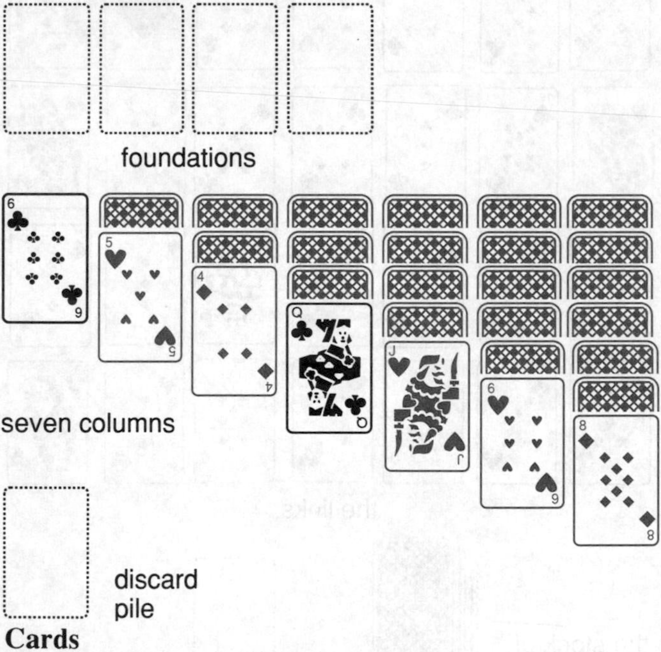

foundations

seven columns

discard pile

Cards

A standard deck of 52 cards is needed.

The layout

Deal one card face up and six more face down in a row from left to right. Along the next row, deal one card face up on the second column and five more face down on the remaining columns, partly overlapping the first row.

Along the next row deal one card face up on the third column and four more face down on the remaining four columns.

Continue in this way until the last column has six face-down cards and one face-up card at the bottom.

The undealt cards are held face down in the hand and form the stock.

Aim

To place the four aces as foundations when they become available during play and to build upon them in suits in ascending order up to K.

Playing

Only one card is played at a time. It can be the top card from the stock or any of the exposed cards from the columns. Any card from the stock which cannot immediately be played is placed face up on a discard pile. The top card of this pile is available for play.

A card may be placed onto an exposed card in the columns, in alternate colours and descending numerical order. Once the foundation aces are relcased during play, cards may then be built onto them in suits in ascending numerical order.

As a card is removed from a column, the next card is turned face up. When a column is used up, its space may only be occupied by a K. The K may be from anywhere in the layout and brings with it any cards already built onto it.

Sequences may be transferred from one column to another as a complete unit.

La Belle Lucie

Cards are placed in fan shapes in this game, creating an attractive layout.

Cards

A standard 52-card deck is needed.

The layout

Deal all the cards face up into 17 fans of three cards each. The remaining card is dealt face up alone.

Aim

To release the four aces as foundations on which to build, in suits and in ascending order, ace up to K.

Playing

The single card and the exposed card of each fan are available to be played. One card at a time is moved either to build onto a foundation, once the aces have been released, or to build numerically downwards on the top card of a fan in the same suit.

Building down onto a fan should be done with care as any cards underneath will be inaccessible. Spaces left by the complete removal of fans are not filled.

Blocked game

When the game becomes blocked because no more cards can be moved, all cards, except those already built onto foundations, are collected and shuffled. They are redealt into fans of three cards plus a pair or a single. Play then continues as before.

If the game becomes blocked again, one more deal takes place, as before. After this second redeal, the first card to be played may be any card on the table. No further redeal takes place.

A sample layout for La Belle Lucie

17 fans and a single card

Monte Carlo

Also known as Double and Quits or Weddings, this game requires players to make pairs.

Cards

A standard deck of 52 cards is needed.

The layout

Four rows of five cards are dealt face up. Players may prefer to play with five rows of five cards.

A sample layout

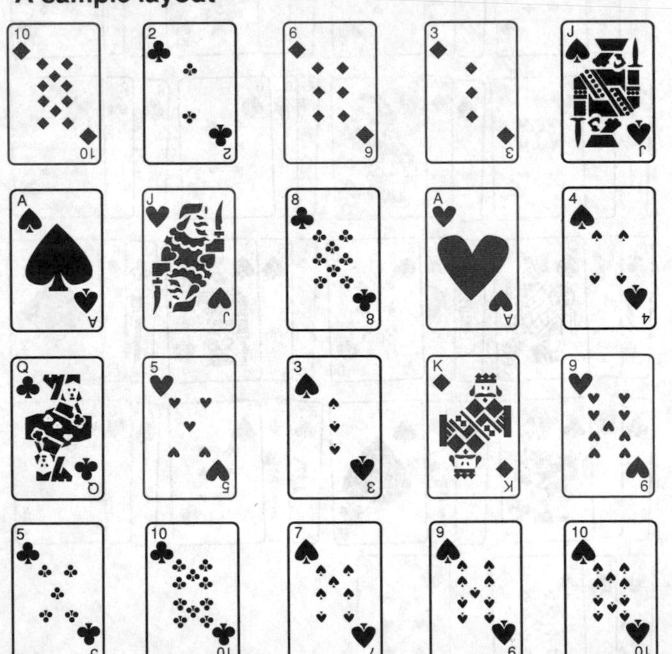

Aim

To clear the table by pairing cards from the layout.

Playing

Any two adjacent cards of the same rank are paired and removed from the layout. The pairing cards may be neighbours at the side, top, bottom or corners.

The spaces are filled by moving the layout cards in the same row to the left, and filling the end space(s) with cards from the row below. The cards should not be rearranged, only moved from right to left or upwards.

After the cards are thus moved, the layout is rebuilt to its starting size with cards from the stock, and further pairing is done.

Play continues until all the cards are paired or until the game is blocked because no more cards can be paired.

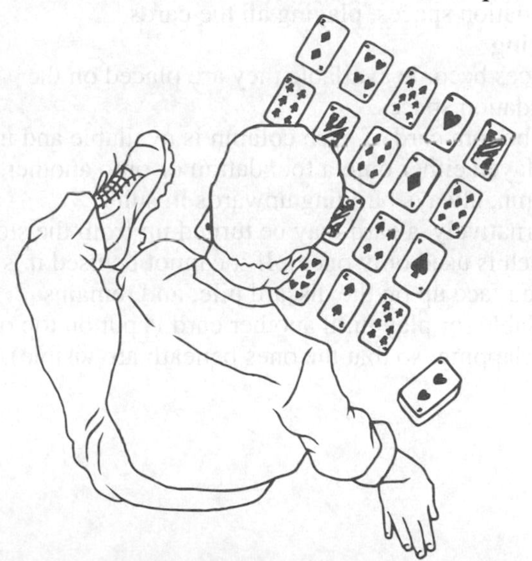

Napoleon at St Helena

Also known as Big Forty and Forty Thieves, this is one of many patience games that may have been played by Napoleon.

Cards

Two standard decks are used, totalling 104 cards.

The layout

Ten cards are dealt face up in a row. Three more rows of ten cards are dealt, each overlapping the last, making ten columns of four overlapping cards. Space will be needed for eight foundations and a discard pile.

Aim

To build upwards from ace to K, in suits, on the eight foundation spaces, playing all the cards.

Playing

As aces become available they are placed on the foundation spaces.

The bottom card of each column is available and may be played either onto a foundation or onto another column, always building upwards in suits.

Alternatively, a card may be turned up from the stock (which is used only once). If it cannot be used it is placed face up on the discard pile, and remains available for play until another card is put on top of it (overlapping, so that the ones beneath are visible).

When a column disappears a new column is begun with any available card. It is best to choose this card with care, keeping in mind its usefulness for bringing others into play.

A sample layout for Napoleon at St Helena

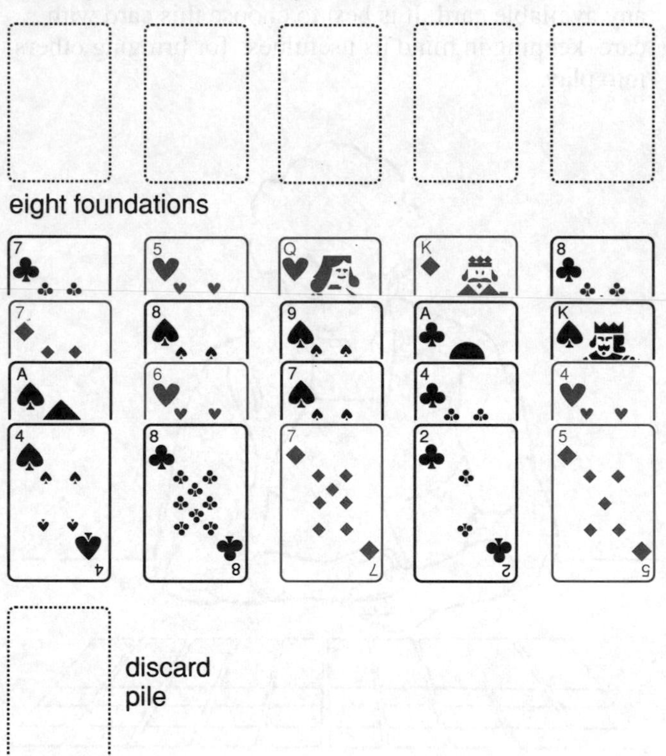

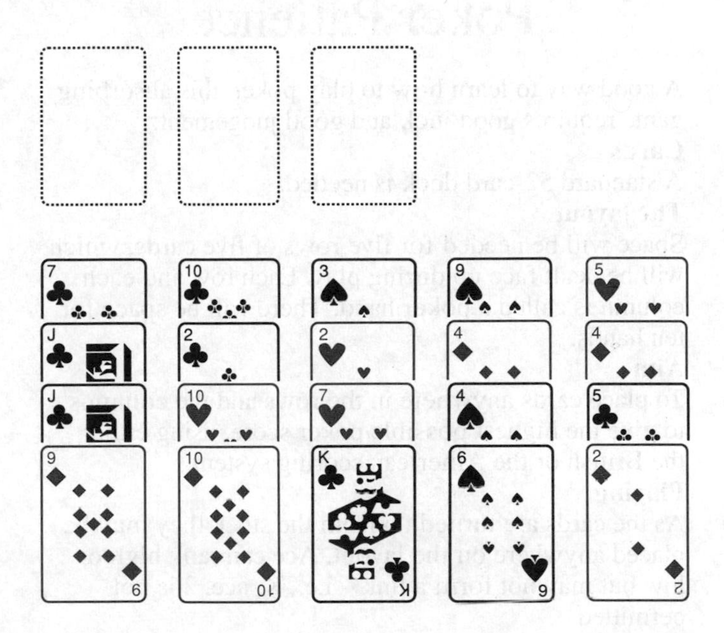

Poker Patience

A good way to learn how to play poker, this absorbing game requires good luck and good judgement.

Cards

A standard 52-card deck is needed.

The layout

Space will be needed for five rows of five cards, which will be dealt face up during play. Each row and each column is called a poker hand. There will be space for ten hands.

Aim

To place cards anywhere in the rows and the columns to give the highest possible poker score, using either the British or the American scoring system.

Playing

As the cards are turned up from the stock they may be placed anywhere on the layout. Ace can rank high or low but may not form a link – i.e., K, ace, 2 is not permitted.

The nine hands

name	combination
royal flush	ace, K, Q, J, 10 of the same suit
straight flush	5-card sequence in same suit
four of a kind	4 cards of one rank + 1 odd
full house	3 same-rank cards + 2 of another rank
flush	5 cards of one suit
straight	any 5-card sequence
three of a kind	3 same-rank cards + 2 odd
two pairs	2 pairs + 1 odd
one pair	1 pair + 3 odd

The layout spaces

The scoring systems

name of hand	American score	British score
royal flush	100	30
straight flush	75	30
four of a kind	50	16
full house	25	10
flush	20	5
straight	15	12
three of a kind	10	6
two pairs	5	3
one pair	2	1
none of the above	0	0

An excellent score would be 200 (American) or 60 (British).

Other rules

1 The joker may be included in the deck and can represent any card. It may simply be added to the stock before dealing or may be used to replace a card after the deal has been played.

2 The 25 cards can be dealt out in the order they are turned up and then can be rearranged to make the best hands.

3 A more difficult variation is to limit the placing of each card to a position neighbouring the last one: side, top, bottom or corner.

Pyramid

This game seems easy, but luck plays a big part.

Cards

A standard 52-card deck is needed.

The layout

A pyramid shape is made by placing cards face up in seven rows, each row one card wider than the one before. Cards overlap leaving only the bottom row of seven cards completely exposed and available at the start of play. Two discard piles are needed.

Aim

To make pairs, using all 52 cards.

Ignoring colour and suit, cards make pairs if their values total 13. Ace is 1, Q 12 and J 11, so an ace and a Q make a pair; so do a J and a 2. Ks are worth 13 and are played alone.

Playing

Play begins by turning up a card from the stock and either pairing it up with an available card from the pyramid or placing it on either discard pile.

Pairs may be made from:

1 the stock card and a pyramid card;

2 two available pyramid cards; or

3 the stock card and the top card of either discard pile.

If the stock pile is exhausted before all cards have been paired, there may be one redeal by collecting both discard piles and using them as the stock pile.

A sample layout for Pyramid

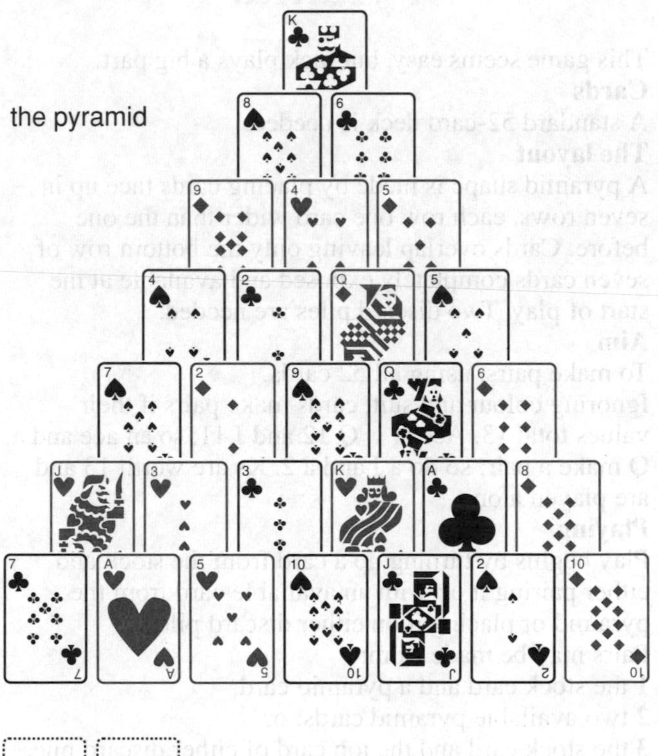

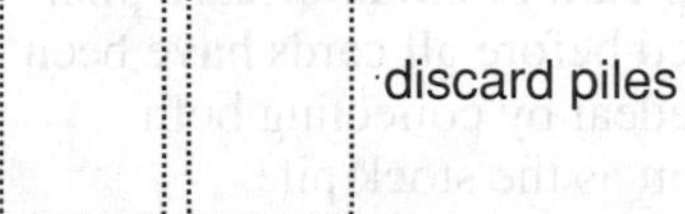

Scorpion

This game does have a sting in its tail because if the hidden cards are not revealed early, they can block further moves towards the end of the game.

Cards

A standard 52-card deck is needed.

The layout

Deal a row of seven cards, the first four face down and the last three face up. Deal two more rows in the same way, each overlapping the previous row. Finally deal four more rows of cards all face up.

The three remaining cards are the reserve and are placed face down below the rows.

The four Ks will be the foundation cards. They are not removed from the layout.

Aim

To build on the Ks in suits in descending order, down to the aces.

Playing

Building can only take place on fully exposed cards – i.e., the bottom card in each column. Any appropriate card in the layout can be used to build and takes with it cards below it in the column. For example, if 4H is exposed, 3H can be built onto it together with all its overlapping cards, as shown overleaf. This move also leaves a Q available for building.

Aces cannot be built on.

The layout for Scorpion

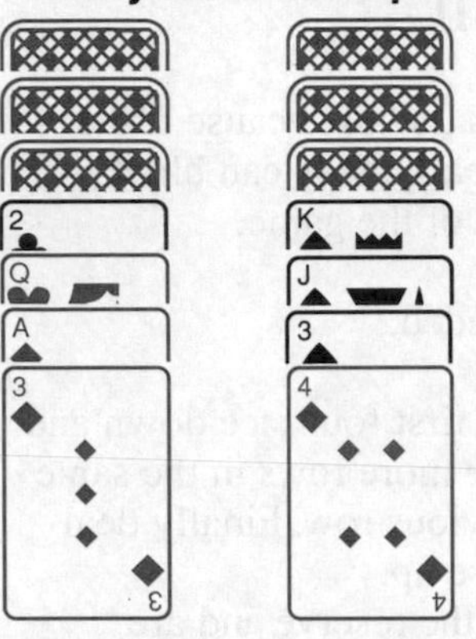

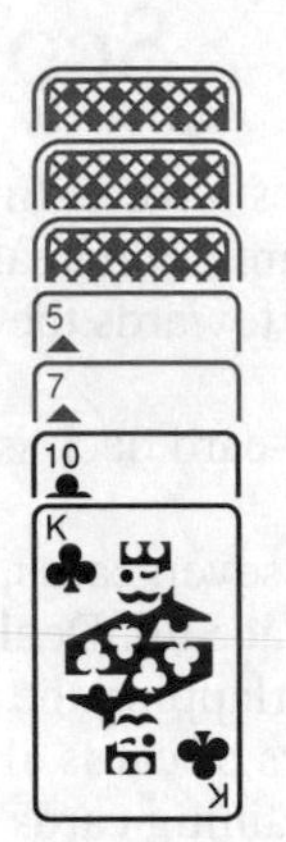

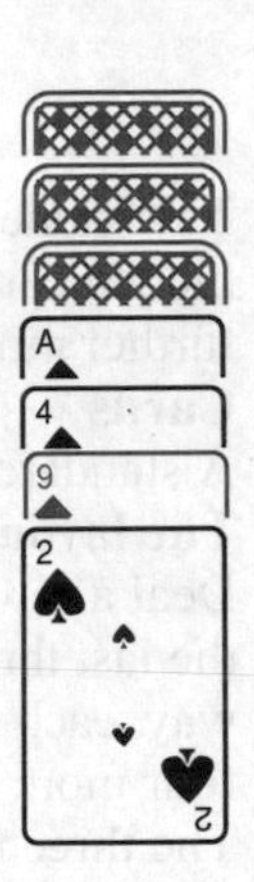

49 cards in seven columns

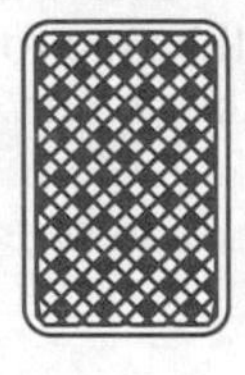

reserve

Example of play

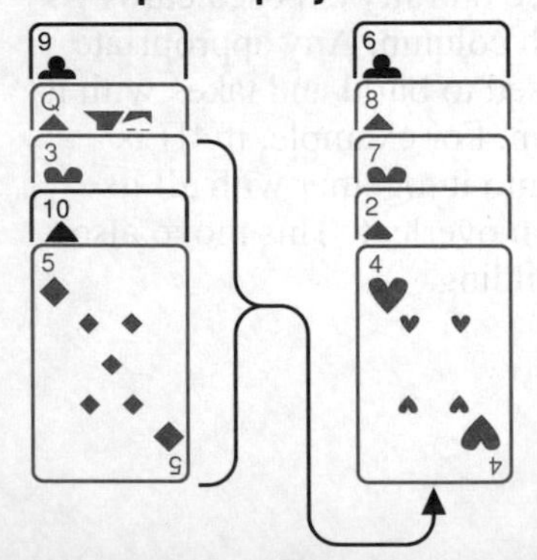

3H is built onto 4H

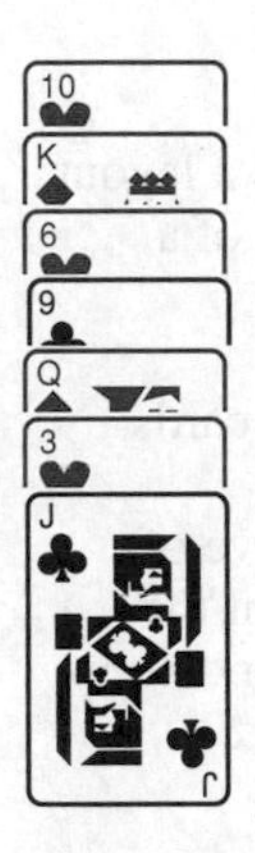

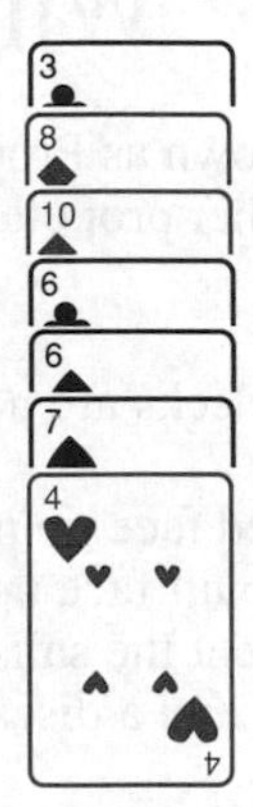

Face-down cards
If a face-down card is exposed, it can then be turned over and is available for play. It is best to try and release the face-down cards early in the game to improve the chances of completing all the building.
Spaces
When a column has been cleared, the space may be filled by a K, plus all the cards below it. Spaces do not have to be filled immediately.
The reserve
Reserve cards are turned up only when no further moves are possible. They can only be added to the bottom of the three left-hand columns. Provided no other moves are possible, the reserve can be turned up before any column spaces are filled, giving the player greater choice.

Windmill

Sometimes known as Propeller, this game has a layout resembling either propeller blades or the sails of a windmill.

Cards

Two standard decks are needed, totalling 104 cards.

The layout

Any K is placed face up in the centre. A reserve of eight cards is built face up, two on each side of the king, to represent the sails. Space for four foundations will be needed and a discard pile.

Aim

There are two aims:

1 to build on the central K, in descending order, regardless of colour or suit. The sequence should consist of 13 cards from K to ace repeated four times to make a total sequence of 52 cards; and

2 to build on the first four aces that become available in ascending order, regardless of suit or colour.

Playing

One card at a time is turned up from the stock and is used either to build or is placed on the discard pile. The first four aces are placed in the foundation spaces in the corners of the "sails".

Cards from the stock, the sails and the top of the discard pile are all available for play onto the four ace foundations and the central K.

In addition, cards from the top of the ace piles can be used to build on the central K. Building on the K helps to resolve the game.

A sample layout with central K

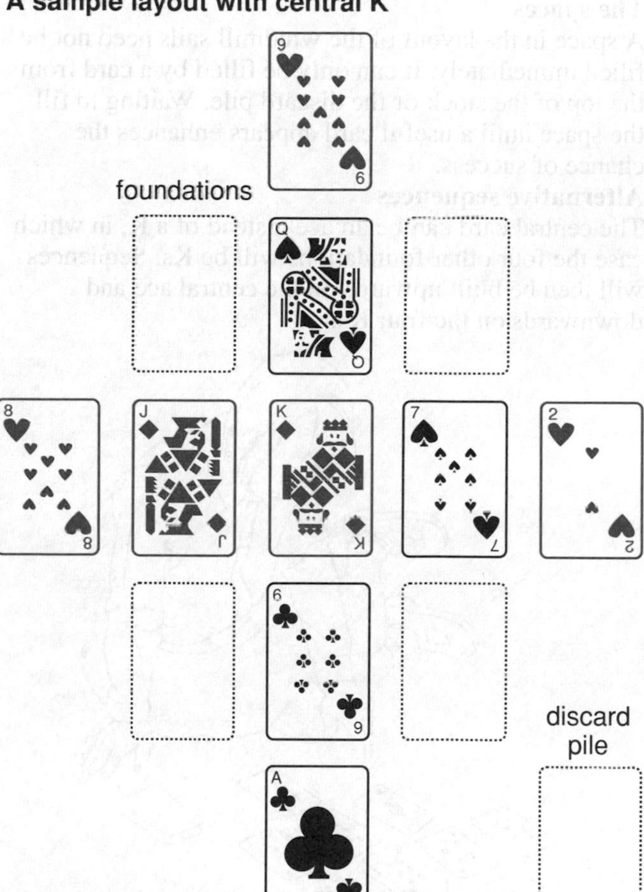

The spaces

A space in the layout of the windmill sails need not be filled immediately. It can only be filled by a card from the top of the stock or the discard pile. Waiting to fill the space until a useful card appears enhances the chance of success.

Alternative sequences

The central card can be an ace instead of a K, in which case the four other foundations will be Ks. Sequences will then be built upwards on the central ace and downwards on the four Ks.

Index

COLLINS POCKET REFERENCE

Other titles in the Pocket Reference series:

Etiquette

A practical guide to what is and what is not acceptable and expected in modern society

Speaking in Public

A guide to speaking with confidence, whatever the occasion

Weddings

How to plan and organize a wedding, from the engagement to the honeymoon

Ready Reference

An invaluable compendium of information on measurements, symbols, codes and abbreviations

What Happened When?

A fascinating source of information for thousands of dates and events

Women's Health

Accessible, quick-reference A-Z guide to the medical conditions which affect women of all ages

COLLINS POCKET REFERENCE

Prescription Drugs

Clear, uncomplicated explanations of prescription drugs and their actions

Letter Writing

A practical guide for anyone who needs to write letters, whether for business or pleasure

Driving Skills

Advice and information on all the skills required by the Driving Test

Office Organizer

A handy guide to all office practices, from ordering stationery to chairing a meeting

Scottish Surnames

A guide to the family names of Scotland